BUILD YOUR OWN

OUTDOOR STRUCTURES

■ IN BRICK ■

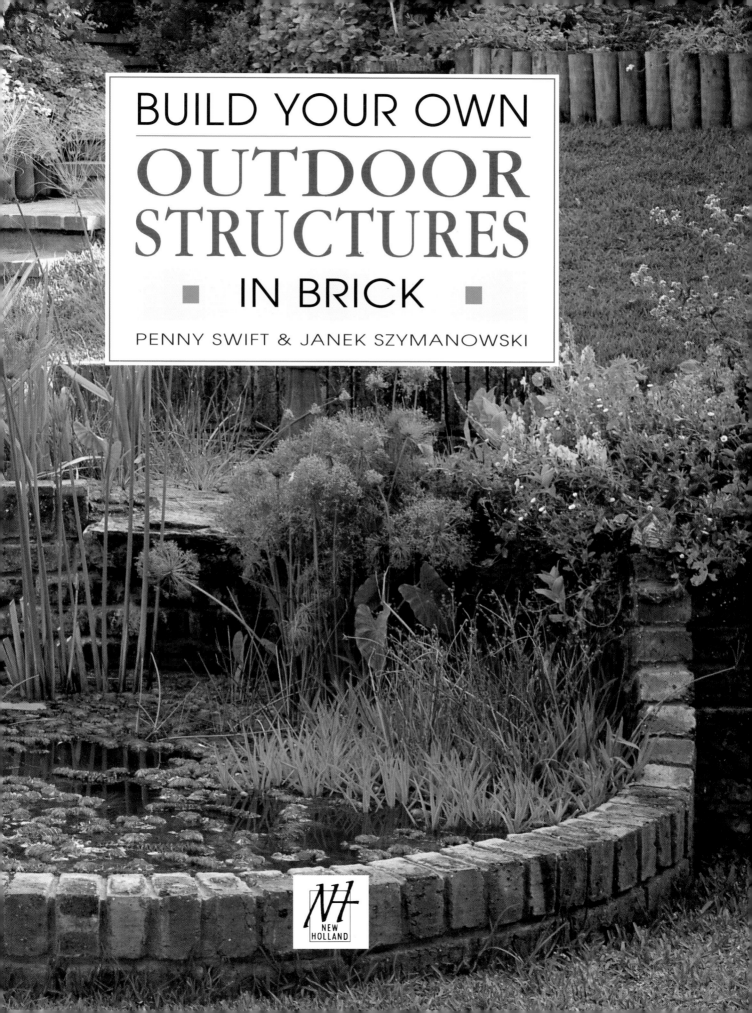

BUILD YOUR OWN

OUTDOOR STRUCTURES

■ IN BRICK ■

PENNY SWIFT & JANEK SZYMANOWSKI

NH
NEW
HOLLAND

ACKNOWLEDGEMENTS

A book of this nature takes time to produce, and there are always a huge number of people to thank when production is complete. Some provide us with locations to photograph, others assist us with the projects. Professionals in various fields also offer advice and share their expertise. We cannot note them all in print, but our gratitude goes to everyone.

This particular title has relied to a large extent on practical information and step-by-step photographs, as well as plans and pictures aimed at inspiring the reader.

Even though we have drawn information from numerous quarters, one company stands out, and a very special thank you must go to Corobrik, manufacturers of clay bricks and maxi-blocks. In particular, we owe our gratitude to Mike Ingram, one of the company's regional directors, who not only organised the projects, but also took time off on weekends to pose for the step-by-step photographs. His enthusiasm and willingness to advise when off duty was inspiring and has undoubtedly helped to make this book a reality.

Several consultants on various continents read the manuscript to ensure international accuracy. We thank them all; but especially Steve Crosswell, regional director of the Portland Cement Institute, and once again, Mike Ingram. It is a challenge to write a book which will appeal to, and relate to people in different parts of the world. These are some of the experts who have made it possible. Thank you.

Finally, we would like to acknowledge the assistance of the publishing team in producing this book.

First published in the UK in 1997 by
New Holland (Publishers) Ltd
London • Cape Town • Sydney • Singapore
24 Nutford Place
London W1H 6DQ

Editors Richard Pooler and Elizé Lübbe
Designers Dean Pollard and Gaelyn Quixley
Cover design Dean Pollard and Gaelyn Quixley
Design assistant Lellyn Creamer
Illustrator Janek Szymanowski

Reproduction by cmyk Prepress, Cape Town
Printed and bound by Tien Wah Press (Pte) Ltd, Singapore

ISBN 1 85368 679 4 (hb)
ISBN 1 85368 741 3 (pb)

CONTENTS

Anyone who values an outdoor lifestyle will appreciate a well-designed garden which incorporates functional areas for entertaining, relaxing or simply sitting outside.

This does not mean that you need a large property; even a small area may be planned to meet the needs of a family that enjoys outdoor living. What you do need, though, are some permanent structures which will facilitate your lifestyle. Built-in seating, tables and barbecue structures will encourage people to spend time outdoors in good weather. A pergola or gazebo will create shelter, a sandpit will provide a place for little children to play, and raised planters, ponds, pools and fountains will all add charm and character to the outdoor space.

While many garden structures are decorative, many more are strictly utilitarian. Simple box-shaped designs, topped with a weatherproof lid, may be used to store firewood, coal or even folding outdoor furniture. A three-sided

enclosure built adjacent to a wall may house rubbish bins, and similar arrangements may be used to make compost, provided the design allows sufficient air to enter the walls.

A pond or fountain may be included in the design of a wall, while steps frequently feature planters on either side. Permanent seating is a welcome addition to any patio.

There are various materials which may be chosen to construct these features, but masonry is undoubtedly the most common, as well as the most durable. Almost all the surviving structures from the ancient world were made from masonry units of some kind, and many of those structures which have disappeared were either destroyed by warfare or demolished by man. Masonry is eminently suitable for all the structures mentioned here; not only will it last well, but it requires relatively little maintenance too.

Although the focus of this book is on brickwork, masonry structures take

many forms, depending on how a specific type of building is used.

Clay bricks (including American adobe mud blocks) are amongst the oldest and most universal materials available. In ancient times, they were simply left in the sun to dry; nowadays, most clay bricks are fired in huge kilns to extremely high temperatures which make them hardy and ideal for all types of building work; size, colour and finish vary from place to place. They can be used in all climatic conditions, and are available all over the world.

Concrete bricks and blocks are a more recent invention, and one which is generally less expensive than clay. Although concrete bricks, moulded to roughly the same size and shape as clay bricks, are solid, the larger blocks are hollow. This makes them easy to work with and simple to reinforce.

Another option is reconstituted or reconstructed stone, also made from concrete (see page 25), but moulded in imitation of natural stone. Not only is this material uniform in size (unlike stone), making it ideal for the do-it-yourself builder, but it is also generally less expensive than the real thing. Of course stone, which is classified as masonry, is perfect for garden structures, and the basic techniques and skills required for bricklaying may be adapted to stonework.

Many people who have never tried working with bricks and mortar find the prospect daunting, but the skills and techniques involved are really not hard to pick up. Learning them takes time and patience, but once you have mastered them, you are sure to find many ways of utilising your new-found abilities to add to and further improve your outdoor environment.

This book will help you understand what is involved, illustrating in a clear, visual manner the skills you will need to master for particular projects. At the same time, it will help you to decide which tasks may be undertaken by

Simple brick pillars form the basic framework for a charming, shady arbour.

others who may be more competent in certain other areas. For instance, you may be more than happy to undertake the physical construction work yourself, but unsure of the technicalities of drawing up plans. If you are unfit, you may prefer to hire labourers to do the more arduous tasks (for instance mixing concrete and mortar) while you tackle those jobs which require a little more expertise. Alternatively (and this is a real option for many people), you may feel your talents lie in organising a team of subcontractors and labourers who will do everything for you. Even members of your family may be prepared to help! But you will still want to be involved in the planning stages of the project, and will benefit from the many suggestions and ideas offered here.

Most of the possibilities given within the pages of this book are minor building projects, but there are still many potential pitfalls and possible obstacles which every do-it-yourselfer should try to avoid. Not only can these threaten to delay the building programme, but they may also add unnecessary costs. Of course, most problems can be avoided with proper planning and a thorough understanding of what is involved. To achieve a professional finish, you should also take a logical approach and follow the project through systematically.

Build Your Own Outdoor Structures in Brick is designed to help you to complete your project successfully, regardless of the specific route you plan to take, and irrespective of how much of the physical work you intend doing yourself. Introductory sections explain basic planning skills and will help you decide what your needs and priorities are, and how to accommodate them. A variety of suitable sites are suggested, along with guidelines that should enable you to establish which is the right location for your own brick structure. Since cost is invariably a vital factor, we suggest ways in which you can cut down on expenditure. There is also information about the various professionals who

Brick has been used to build planters, a garden seat and a simple barbecue unit.

may be able to help you in certain areas, and a useful section which examines the kinds of regulations and building codes which may affect your particular project.

A host of design ideas is provided and explained in layman's terms, enabling anyone to create an attractive feature which blends with their existing outdoor environment. The importance of using compatible materials is highlighted, and the relevance of harmony and balance, along with the significance of size and proportion, are considered in a straightforward manner. A breakdown of the possibilities which may be explored when using bricks and blocks of various kinds is given, and a range of style options is recommended. Since even a simple brick pergola or gazebo may incorporate a roof of some sort, numerous suitable roofing materials are assessed, as is a comprehensive range of masonry building units.

For those wanting to tackle more complicated projects, there is some

basic information on extensions and additions, as well as a detailed look at what is involved in creating an outdoor kitchen or a barbecue. Traditional garden buildings, including plant houses and utility structures, are also discussed.

The full spectrum of tools and materials required for bricklaying are itemised and some helpful hints given regarding how to assess quantities correctly. Although the emphasis in this book is obviously on brickwork, the preparation and use of concrete, which is essential for foundations, is also discussed briefly. Basic building methods, essential principles of construction and the best techniques are then explained.

In a separate step-by-step section, these building methods are illustrated succinctly in photographic form. The aim here is not to follow through one project as such, but to present a hands-on sample of the techniques which you will need to tackle the range of plans presented on pages 52–61.

Any project which involves the construction of a permanent feature must be well planned. If it is not, you are likely to waste time and money. You should assess your needs carefully and consider exactly what function your brick structure is to fulfil. You can then decide exactly where to site the feature and establish how much assistance will be required. Before you go any further, you will also need to cost the project and ensure that you are able to fund it fully. It pays to plan properly right from the start. If you are systematic and thorough, the entire project should run smoothly and you will be proud of the end result.

YOUR NEEDS
Every homeowner's needs are different, and only you can decide what will suit your own and your family's circumstances.

A major element to consider at the outset is your lifestyle. If you entertain frequently and favour the alfresco approach in good weather, you will probably need a fairly elaborate arrangement which might include an outdoor kitchen with storage areas. Seating and built-in tables are also options worth considering. Perhaps you and your family spend as much time as possible outdoors, soaking up the sun and enjoying the fresh air. In addition to the practical functions of seating and cooking facilities, you may also want to consider decorative features like planters and ponds which will improve the general appearance of a patio or courtyard. Of course, a permanent masonry structure will be part of the general garden design, but it must be planned with your needs at heart, even if you decide to employ a professional to devise an outdoor scheme for you.

If you are an indoor person, but your living room overlooks a spot which will benefit from similarly ornamental features, your needs will be slightly different. For instance, you may love the sound of trickling water, in which case a fountain should be positioned so that it can be both seen and heard from inside the house.

Your children may spend more time outdoors than you do, and a little-used patio could become a favourite play area if given the benefit of a plant-covered pergola for shade. You could perhaps build a brick-sided sandpit at one end for toddlers, or a simple lean-to, comprising a low wall which supports roof sheeting, to provide an all-weather play shelter for older children. This could even become a storage facility for bicycles and other recreational items.

In the garden itself, you may want features such as planters, steps, raised ponds and walled beds, depending on the layout of the area. Pergolas and solid brick arches may also be required as a part of the general design.

Do not forget to consider the utility areas, especially if you want to hide rubbish bins or if you like to pack compost into a neat enclosure.

Finally, think about any immediate needs which may change. Make absolutely certain you can adapt the plan to accommodate change.

CHOOSING THE RIGHT SITE
Brick structures, however low or small, cannot be moved, so it is essential to make certain that they are sited correctly. Mistakes can be expensive – if not impossible – to rectify.

The type of feature or structure you are planning to build will largely determine where it is to be located. Built-in benches, for instance, will usually be used to their full potential if constructed on a patio. Presuming that you have an established patio, or have pinpointed an area where you plan to build one, you will need to determine exactly where to place the seating. Ideally it should be reasonably sheltered from prevailing winds, and positioned to take advantage of a view, either beyond the garden or within its confines. However, you may want seating away from the house; perhaps

An expansive patio, shaded by a brick-piered pergola, may be used for several activities.

in a rose or herb garden, or alongside a trickling stream (if you are lucky enough to have one meandering through your garden).

Similarly, a structure intended for outdoor cooking will normally be sited on a patio – more often than not, quite close to the house. Alternatively, you can build it up against a boundary wall which screens the site from the wind, or alongside an outbuilding which offers storage space.

The most sensible approach is to scrutinise every possible location and to then look at the advantages and disadvantages of each. Make a list and note down your preferences in relation to the function of the structure and your needs.

If you are starting from scratch, sit down with a piece of paper and a pencil and sketch some ideas. It is preferable to use graph paper to help you work to scale. Mark all the established features and buildings, trees, large rocks and even shrubs which you want to retain. Then draw in the basic framework of walls, hedges, paths and patios, and identify any definable activity centres (a utility area for washing lines, a vegetable or herb garden, an entertainment patio, play area and so on). Note the direction of prevailing winds and spots which get more than average sun or shade.

Accessibility

An important factor for almost any structure in the garden is accessibility which will, to a large degree, determine its usefulness. If you cannot get to a raised planter with ease, you will tend to neglect the plants and flowers growing in it; if you have to plough through shrubs to reach a seat, there is little point in having the structure, even if it has been built to capture a stunning view; if a masonry gazebo is positioned so that one has to climb a steep flight of steps to get to it, its usefulness will be limited to a hideaway only for those who are fit enough to reach it!

Visibility

It stands to reason that a primarily decorative feature must be sited where

Built-in seating combines well with a precast table in a small, intimate outdoor eating area.

A two-tiered pond built out of facebrick is an ideal design for a sloping garden.

During the planning phase, before any major decisions are made and money is spent, it is essential to check legalities with your local council or building department. Most will require plans and specifications for any masonry structure, and there may be limitations in terms of what and where you may build.

If you go ahead without the necessary approval, you could find yourself having to demolish the fruits of your labour. Furthermore, there may be other penalties like a hefty fine.

Remember that a primary motivation for establishing these codes and regulations relates to safety: your local authority wants to be sure that structures are sound and will not collapse.

Although specific requirements and details will differ depending on where you live, it is possible to generalise in terms of the type of standards set internationally. Many of these relate to what may simply be considered 'good building practice'.

You will find that there are various minimum requirements relating to foundations, the height of various structures, drainage and so on. There are also minimum specifications regarding materials (particularly when these are structural elements), while other rules relate to boundaries, building lines and certain zoning laws.

Of course not all of these specifications will relate to brickwork, and even fewer to garden brickwork. But it is vital to find out which codes and regulations will affect you.

If you are required to present working drawings, you will probably have to submit a site plan indicating boundaries, building lines, existing buildings and any major feature like a swimming pool or shed, all clearly shown in relation to the existing structures. Proposed new work will usually be coloured on the plan. These colours are specific and must relate to the materials which are to be used (masonry,

timber, concrete and so on). You may also have to indicate the contours of the site, as well as present sections and elevations to illustrate the proposed structure. Drainage installations may also have to be shown, along with any structures you wish to demolish.

If you plan to build on a boundary, it may be necessary to get written consent from the affected neighbours before your proposals can be considered by the authorities. If a building permit is required, you will need to pay the prescribed fee before work can begin.

Most local authorities and councils will provide a checklist of what is required; an architect or draughtsman will be familiar with these criteria.

If your house is old and you do not have the plans, consult the relevant authorities before employing somebody to draw these up from scratch. The originals will most likely be on file and you will be able to obtain copies.

Most local authorities require plans and an outline of specifications for any brick structures to be constucted in the garden.

A well-constructed brick patio with walled sides offers shelter from both sun and wind.

t can be seen to best advantage. A strictly utilitarian structure, on the other hand, should be positioned out of view. If you are building something which is practical, but will be located on a patio or near to an entrance, you will need to ensure that it is also an attractive feature. A barbecue is a good example, as frequent use tends to blacken the walls and it can become an eyesore. Siting it away from the house can be inconvenient, and even if it is linked to a patio, the cook may be left to do the dirty work alone. A little camouflage, with potted plants, clay ornaments and other weatherproof items can save the day though.

Conditions
The microclimate of your garden is another important factor to consider. Prevailing winds are an obvious consideration when siting built-in benches and other alfresco eating and cooking structures. It is preferable to chose a sheltered spot, and one that will not become damp and cold – you will want to get the maximum possible use from these features.

Planters should also be reasonably protected from wind and, in hot climates, from the sun as well. Take full advantage of existing walls and

screens and note the spots where trees provide natural shelter.

COST
Cost is a factor that cannot be ignored, and can put a damper on any project. With careful planning and conscientious

budgeting, though, you can keep costs reasonable and wastage to a minimum. The first step is to establish what kind of outlay you will have to make to be able to build the features you are planning. Try to be as accurate as possible. Avoid guesswork for even the most minor projects and gather as much information as you can.

If you already have plans, you should be able to quantify the materials required relatively easily. Otherwise, sketch the proposed structure to scale and then work out what you will need, following the guidelines given on pages 32–37.

You will need to estimate the total area of all the brickwork, which will give an indication of the number of bricks needed. If the structure is to be rendered, the area will also determine how much cement, lime and sand will be called for; the number of bricks will be the determining factor in terms of cement, lime and sand for bricklaying. You will then need to work out what is required for the concrete foundation (see page 37).

Since there is always some wastage (bricks get broken and sand blows

A raised pond has been situated in the centre of a courtyard to create a focal point.

Paving can be laid by the DIYer, but larger structures are best done with professional help.

If you feel you cannot tackle the building work yourself, a building contractor, or even a bricklayer, may be the person whose help you require. Otherwise you may just want to employ a labourer to help you.

Before you employ anybody, find out what their qualifications are, check that they are properly licensed (where applicable), and ask to see examples of their work. If possible, visit some of the sites on which they have worked and talk to the owners. Also establish exactly how they plan to go about the job. If, for instance, you are hiring someone to undertake the entire operation, check whether this person plans to subcontract a portion of the job (the actual building, for instance). In such a case it may be cheaper for you to consider other options.

away), you should order slightly more of each material than you think you will need. Do not forget to add this extra amount into the initial costings. Order about 5–10% more than you have calculated and this should cover you.

If additional materials are to be used, for instance for roofing or storage areas, these must also be costed, along with any labour you are planning to employ. Professional fees (if any) should also be included.

All sorts of items can increase the costs, but if you know exactly what is required, you can budget accordingly. You may even be able to stagger the project and complete it as additional funds become available.

PROFESSIONAL ASSISTANCE

Unless you have some kind of building experience, there is a good chance you will need the assistance of at least one professional. Since plans are often required for masonry structures, the person who is most likely to draw these up will be a draughtsman or architect who can formalise your ideas on paper and ensure that they are acceptable to the authorities in your area. If the features you are planning are part of an integrated landscape scheme, you may decide to use the services of a landscape architect.

Even a relatively simple brick walkway or pergola usually requires plans before you can build.

Architect and architectural designer

An advantage of employing an architect or designer to tackle garden brickwork projects is that he or she has been trained in building styles, and will be able to create an effect which blends with the existing house and outbuildings on your property. Often a short consultation is all that is required and you can then approach a draughtsman (see below) to draw up any required plans. Architects will usually tackle this type of project only if they were involved with the initial design of the house. It is usually a better idea to consult a landscape architect who specialises in gardens and other outdoor areas.

Landscape architect and landscaper

The types of brick structure considered here are very much a part of garden design and landscaping as a whole. It is therefore advisable to seek the services of somebody who specialises in this field. Bear in mind that a landscape architect has a professional qualification, while many 'landscapers' may simply be garden specialists with varying amounts of knowledge and experience rather than formal training. Who you decide to use will depend on your needs and the abilities and expertise of the professionals available in your area.

Draughtsman

Architects and designers frequently subcontract draughtsmen to draw up their plans for them. If you know what you want, you could instead contact one directly to do the same for you. Most draughtsmen have a working knowledge of the materials required as well as the specifications set down by the local authority.

Make sure that you approach the right person before you go ahead and spend money on plans.

Building contractor

Usually many builders are available to undertake garden brickwork projects, but not all of them are competent. Make absolutely certain you have reliable recommendations and inspect

A brick pergola and adjoining wall have been designed to match the style of the house.

work completed by the builder you plan to use. Also check that he is in a position to submit plans on your behalf (if these are required). If he is not, the chances are that he is simply subcontracting labour and does not have an established business. Before signing any agreements, confirm whether the building contractor will provide all the materials; if you are able to source cheaper materials it is possible to cut costs by agreeing to a labour-only contract.

Some building companies specialise in specific types of structure, including pergolas, carports, gazebos and barbecues. If any of these features fit into your design scheme, you may want to get quotations from the companies offering them. Again, it is wise to check how much of the project they will complete themselves, and also to compare their quotation with the cost of doing the job yourself.

Subcontractor

A number of trained workmen, including bricklayers and stonemasons, may be hired for the job. Most will charge an hourly fee, although you may be able to set a fee for the entire project. You will have to supervise the work yourself and it is therefore essential that you have a basic understanding of all the procedures involved.

Locating competent subcontractors can be difficult, although you can often rely on verbal referrals from friends or neighbours who have recently had building work done. Alternatively, check the classified advertisements in your local newspaper, but don't forget to ask for references.

It is a good idea to check the legal implications of hiring casual labour. In some areas you will need to observe certain labour regulations, and other requirements such as insurance under Workers' Compensation.

A neat brick plinth beneath a garden lamp.

Good design is an essential element of any garden scheme. Not only must the brick structures you are planning blend with the architectural style and finish of your house, but they must also suit the garden environment in which they are to be located. It is important that larger features do not block sunlight or spoil a vista, and that nothing looks as though it is an afterthought which was built in a rush.

There are so many design options for masonry structures that it can be confusing to those without expreience. But if you follow a few basic rules, and rely on common sense, you will find that it is really not that difficult to create something which is both practical and visually pleasing.

If you get stuck, reconsider the possibility of seeking professional guidance at this early stage.

DESIGN BASICS

An excellent starting point is to consider the garden as an extension of the house. Not only will this give you an idea of suitable materials for garden buildings, features and small structures of all types, but it will also guide you in terms of size, scale and proportion. It may even suggest a suitable style for your structure.

The kind of garden you have serves as a guide. If it is essentially formal, with straight lines and clearly defined beds, brickwork should also be formal. An informal garden with curved paths,

A low brick planter alongside the house has been rendered to match the walls of the building.

natural rockeries and island beds will benefit from a less austere approach. Seating may be curved, or simply interspersed with planters to create a more harmonious effect, and ponds built in an irregular shape. The design of a structure which features straight lines and square corners (and by the very nature of brickwork, many do), may be softened by planting or placing pots on or around it.

Balance and proportion

A variety of elements are found in outdoor areas, big and small. These range from trees, shrubs and flowers, to the vast array of structures which may be built from masonry. One of the fundamental principles of good design is that balance is created between all these components. Furthermore, they must be combined so that there is harmony between what nature provides and what we are able to construct ourselves.

If there is too much brickwork and it is not softened by plants, it will tend to look out of place, incongruous and unbalanced. If any structure is not in proportion to the garden (or patio) and the house, it will look discordant; if it is simply too large, and out of proportion, it will be too dominant and will ruin the whole effect.

Contrast

Contrast is another fundamental requirement within the garden, but it should not be obtrusive or obvious. Instead, it should be used to introduce a kind of pattern and texture. There are various ways of achieving this, but one of the most obvious is to combine hard elements (including brickwork) with soft landscaping or planting. Not only are the walls of a structure juxtaposed with natural elements found outdoors, but they can be softened further by planting along the base, or by the addition of built-in containers as part of the design.

Various structures will introduce shadows into the garden, and this in itself is a form of contrast. For instance, the beams of a pergola will create a pattern of straight lines across

Built-in brick furniture should be in proportion with the size of the patio area.

A neat facebrick letterbox matches the style of other brick structures in the front garden.

the ground when the sun shines, while a series of archways will introduce an uneven play of light and shade.

Colour, too, can create contrasts, with facebrick surfaces adding earthy shades and textures to green leaves and bushes.

SIZE AND SCALE

Having established the importance of proportion in the garden plan as a whole, it follows that any masonry structure you decide to build should be designed to a suitable scale. If it is not,

the scheme will lack balance and unity. Generally, the size of any design should complement the house and the garden. However there are not many unbreakable rules in garden design, and you will need to assess how the brick structure you plan to build will fit into the available space you have.

It seems obvious that minimal structures fit small spaces and that you need a large property to build something on a grand scale. While this is a safe and obvious route for most people to follow, it is also possible

A carefully planned brick patio incoporates a pergola, built-in seating and a cooking area.

Red brick has been used to create harmony on a patio with several permanent structures.

to create cosy corners alongside a mansion, and you may well be able to build an expansive outdoor entertainment area beside a little cottage without it looking odd. In the latter instance, you will need to consider the scale of pergola pillars, built-in seating and any other brick features very carefully. Built-in seating around the entire perimeter of a large patio which adjoins a small dwelling will make the area look like a public arena, while an enormous barbecue with a towering chimney will simply look out of place. Designing small features which mirror the size and scale of the house can also be a problem if the hard (or paved) surface of the patio is relatively vast. The answer may be to aim for a focal point in one section of the patio. In this way you may be able successfully to create a series of features in this area.

Apart from the relative sizes of the buildings and other structures on your property, it is also important to consider what various features will look like from several vantage points, both inside and outside the house. Avoid any design which may reduce the amount of sunlight reaching the interior of your house, or a structure which obscures an attractive view or vista across the garden.

If you want to build something in order to block an ugly outlook, your approach will, naturally, be quite different. Perhaps you are planning to erect a screen wall with a decorative fountain in brick. This should be positioned not only to hide the offending outlook, but to be an attractive feature as well.

Some brick structures, including feature walls, pergolas and walkways, may be used to divide the garden at certain points. A clever design, constructed near the boundary, may even create the impression that the garden continues a lot further than it actually does. Adapting the Japanese concept of optical illusion will enable you to build a feature on a larger scale that might otherwise have seemed inappropriate, as the garden will seem to continue beyond the structure.

A bar counter alongside a built-in barbecue doubles as storage for several appliances.

While a patio designed for entertaining may simply comprise a paved surface with seating and perhaps a pergola for shade, an outdoor kitchen requires a lot more detail, including the need for cooking and storage facilities.

The basic elements of designing a barbecue structure are discussed on page 20. By extending the plan to include additional features, you will certainly increase its usefulness.

There are numerous features you can include in an outdoor kitchen. Instead of a barbecue unit where food is always cooked over the coals, consider a simple spit or battery-operated rotisserie. These are readily available and will increase the range of dishes you can cook. Pizza ovens and smaller baking ovens are other options, although you will need to be sure you have adequate bricklaying skills to tackle these projects. Unless properly constructed, with the inclusion of fire bricks, a chimney and, in the case of a baking oven, a solid door, they will not work properly. You may also consider incorporating a warming plate to keep meals hot.

One of the most important design details of any barbecue unit is the fire bed, where cooking takes place. It is essential that this surface can withstand the intense heat of the fire, or you could find the whole structure cracking and even collapsing. The first step is to ensure that the surface where the fire will be made is flat and stable. While there is nothing to stop you from using the upper surface of a solid structure built to the required height, this will be wasted brickwork, unless, perhaps, the barbecue is built into an adjacent wall.

Instead, most designs feature a fire bed over an open area between the side walls of the structure. This is an ideal space for storing firewood, especially if the unit has an enclosed back wall as well. You can use a reinforced precast or galvanised steel lintel to span the space, or a precast concrete slab; otherwise you could cast concrete using shuttering (formwork), which ideally should be reinforced as well.

Once this is in place, the secret is to top the concrete with a material which will not crack once a fire has been lit. Clay bricks or pavers, which are fired to very high temperatures during the manufacturing process, are ideal. Alternatively you can use special fire bricks, although these are relatively costly and not really necessary if good quality clay bricks are available. You could also top the slab with a buffer layer of soft sand, and then fit a metal ash tray, similar to those used for some indoor fireplaces. The advantage of these is that they can be removed whenever you want to clean up the coals, so you avoid having to sweep the coals off a fixed brick surface.

Other fittings also simplify the task of cooking outdoors. For instance, some people favour the inclusion of gas or electrical supplies and even a sink unit alongside the working surface. If these connections are to be provided, they should be supplied by licensed professionals; it is a relatively easy task, however, to install the necessary conduiting and pipework.

While many barbecue structures are located out in the open, elaborate designs are usually more successful in a sheltered spot on the patio; the site you choose will depend on your needs and on the options available on your property.

A bricked-in precast pond is tiled for effect.

This simple brick structure incorporates seating, a small side table, planter and screen wall

TYPE

The range of brick structures suitable for a garden, courtyard or patio is limited only by your imagination, your budget and the practical consideration of your building skills. Although bricklaying skills are easy to acquire, an amateur bricklayer who has never tackled a project before is advised to stick to something simple. If you take it one step at a time, you may eventually master even the most elaborate design. At the other end of the scale, an engineer who wants to do a bit of DIY can probably set his sights a little higher, with a greater knowledge of the principles and techniques involved.

The range of ideas that follow are aimed to appeal to a wide spectrum of do-it-yourselfers; it is up to you to set the limits.

Planters

A brick planter is one of the simplest projects to tackle and as a feature it can be very effective, transforming a stark patio almost literally overnight.

In a flat, uninteresting garden, a series of planters will enable you to create raised or even tiered levels or to divide a boring space, in this way creating interest and form. If you plant large foliage plants, you will eventually create an attractive screen, while flowers will add a splash of colour.

In cases where you are faced with the prospect of a long, plain wall, either on the boundary or within the garden itself, the addition of planters in the design will immediately create visual interest. They may also be included in the layout of an outdoor stairway, or built on either side of a couple of steps, possibly at the entrance to the house or the approach to a garden terrace.

In an elaborate patio design, planters may also feature alongside built-in seating, tables or a barbecue structure. Planted with striking or colourful species, a planter can become the principal decorative feature of an area.

Far easier to maintain than pots and other free-standing containers, built-in planters are particularly useful in areas with inferior soil conditions. They are also useful where drainage is a problem, because the base may be filled with broken bricks and stones, and weepholes or drainage pipes incorporated to lead water away from the roots of the plants.

Since quality soil of any type may be used to fill a planter, you can often introduce species which would not usually thrive in the environment of your garden. You must be sure, though, that the dimensions of the container are suitable for the plants

you choose. Large shrubs or trees with spreading roots should be avoided.

Water features

Bricks and blocks are ideal materials for the construction of formal ponds and fountain features. They may be used to build up the sides of water features, raising them above ground level, so that floating and marginal plants as well as fish and other creatures are easier to locate and watch. Alternatively, a low pond (possibly only one or two bricks high) may form a basin below a wall which has been fitted with a gargoyle or some other fountain head. You may even consider the possibility of a wishing well, particularly if you live in a quaint cottage.

An imaginative design may include planters or even adjacent seating which will provide a place to view the fish. Sometimes the edge of the pool itself may double as an informal seating area. This is particularly suited to an ornamental Nishikigoi or koi pond where the colours and shapes of the fish are the attractive focal point.

Masonry may also be used to construct informal ponds, but natural stone or reconstituted stone blocks are generally more suitable materials than bricks as they have a much less formal appearance.

A major factor when building water features in brick is the question of waterproofing. If the inner surface is not properly sealed, the pond or pool will leak. The most effective procedure is to render the inner surface with mortar, to which a waterproofing compound has been added, and then to paint on bitumen or some other suitable nontoxic sealant.

The outside of a brick pond may also be rendered, depending on the effect you wish to create.

Seating and built-in furniture

Any furniture intended to be left outside permanently must be made from a material which will last and not deteriorate in wet or other extreme conditions. Masonry is therefore an obvious choice. It can be combined with other materials, including timber, which makes a sensible but attractive surface for both seats and tables. Alternatively, brickwork can be filled in and the tops of some furniture designs can be tiled, topped with concrete or reconstituted stone slabs, or even finished with brick paving.

The location of permanent outdoor furniture will depend on your personal requirements. For example, you may want somewhere to relax away from the house, or perhaps a place where family and friends can go as a retreat away from the house, for a drink or meal, without having to lug chairs and stools with them.

Some types of movable furniture may be left outside in all weather, but built-in benches and tables are a very useful addition to a patio. The simplest designs comprise supporting walls which provide a base for table tops and timber seating. Set against a wall, a bench will automatically have a back and all you will need is a few cushions to provide a comfortable place to relax; you can simply remove them when the furniture is not in use.

There is no reason why furniture constructed in brick should not be located in the garden itself. A bench tucked away in a corner which faces colourful flower beds, a rose garden or a water feature, will encourage you to spend time enjoying these visual

An elaborate patio design with built-in furniture and a practical barbecue shelf is ideal for home-cooked meals and entertaining.

A plastered brick barbecue is a feature on a brick-paved patio.

pleasures. If the bench is topped with a material like granite or mosaic, it will become a feature in its own right.

The size and dimensions of outdoor furniture will depend on the function you expect it to fulfil. A long bench, for instance, will require intermediate supporting pillars to prevent the seat from sagging.

If a table is located alongside seating, it is important to ensure that the height of the seat is compatible with the height of the table top. Seating should be close enough to the ground to enable feet to rest comfortably on the surface below, while the table should be positioned in such a way that it can be used for meals and with sufficient space to get in behind it.

Benches may be built in on either side of a table, or you can use portable seating on one side. The latter option can be more versatile if you entertain regularly, since you can vary the seating arrangement and the table will also be accessible for buffet meals.

Seating arrangements do not have to be elaborate; even a single timber-topped seat alongside a pond or planter can be both functional and aesthetically pleasing.

Barbecue structures

Anybody who enjoys an alfresco meal is sure to delight in the opportunity to cook outdoors. People all over the world enjoy meals prepared over an open fire, using a variety of both portable and permanent units. If the idea appeals to you, a built-in barbecue will add an enjoyable element to outdoor entertaining.

Ideally, the structure will include a reasonable working surface (even if you prepare the food in the kitchen, you will want somewhere to put dishes and plates), seating and storage space for firewood, cooking implements and maybe gas bottles.

The design you choose will depend not only on your requirements and the environment in which it is to be

located, but also on your building skills. A simple arrangement will involve little more than constructing a series of walls, and once you have mastered basic bricklaying, you should have no difficulty with it. Incorporating a chimney takes a little more experience and ability, and the addition of an oven (either for pizzas or for baking bread) demands considerable expertise. Make sure you are familiar with all the techniques required before you tackle a project which could become arduous.

Siting a barbecue correctly is important as it will affect the use you get out of it. It should be out of the wind, accessible to the house (in particular the kitchen), and positioned near a seating area where family and friends are likely to gather. Avoid locating it anywhere near large trees as overhanging branches may be damaged by the fire.

Smoke is inevitably a problem, particularly on a confined or partially enclosed patio, but this can be minimised by an efficient chimney which will draw smoke away from the area.

Storage units and garden utilities

Surprisingly few people consider the advantage of building simple storage units on patios or in the garden. Those that are most common occur in utility areas and are used to house or screen rubbish bins, store swimming pool equipment or shelter coal and firewood. They are generally plain, unexciting and sometimes rather unattractive items which do nothing to improve the appeal of the outdoor area.

Imaginatively planned, outdoor storage for cushions, barbecue equipment such as gas bottles, pool items and even smaller gardening implements (hand spade, secateurs, gloves and so on) may be incorporated in the patio plan. All that is needed is a watertight box with a securely fitting lid, shelving which is sheltered from the elements, or a right-angled wall which could incorporate a planter to screen a rubbish bin. If you are building a barbecue, consider fronting

TRADITIONAL GARDEN STRUCTURES

Since stone is a natural material and brick has been used for thousands of years, it is not surprising that many traditional garden structures and buildings are built with various types of masonry.

Garden houses of earlier ages were built in brick or stone in some parts of the world, like England and Europe, and in wood in 18th century America. Garden structures were a feature of the gardens of the wealthy, their styles varying from country to country and changing through the ages. The ancient Romans were known to have used marble for some of their garden houses, and some beautiful banqueting houses, used purely for entertaining, were built from local stone in England during the Tudor period. Often these were sited at some distance from the house and used either for banquets or as a secret retreat from the world.

Follies, which enjoyed their heyday in 18th century Britain, were also built from masonry units, most frequently stone. These took various forms, from temples and pyramids to structures deliberately made to look like ruined buildings. They had no real use except to catch the eye and perhaps to act as a temporary shelter for visitors touring the property. These too, were found only in the gardens of the wealthy, but smaller versions were designed by a number of Victorian garden landscapers.

One of the most charming garden buildings of the 19th century was built by the renowned British garden designer, Gertrude Jekyll. Known as The Thunder House (and designed by the equally renowned architect, Sir Edwin Lutyens), it is a plain gazebo-like structure built from local stone (as was the house), and was often used in Miss Jekyll's day to watch the progress of summer thunder storms!

The gazebo is perhaps the most time-honoured garden structure. Built from stone or brick, it was traditionally sited at one corner of a property or on a terrace, and was often raised so that it could capture the view beyond. Designed in a square, hexagonal or octagonal shape, the gazebo generally features a steeply pitched roof which was traditionally covered with slate, shingles or sometimes thatch.

There are much-photographed traditional gazebos all over the world, many of which have survived for hundreds or even thousands of years. Apart from Gertrude Jekyll's Thunder House, another famous design was by an American, Lawrence Johnston, who built a square, brick gazebo with a shingled roof in the garden of his Hidcote Manor home in England.

Summerhouses too, were frequently built from stone or brick. More reclusive and less open than a gazebo, a summerhouse was the place to sit on warm summer days. Although today's summerhouse is often used for temporary accommodation, the traditional type was generally too open and offered only partial shelter. By the mid-19th century, wood was a more common material than masonry for this kind of structure.

On a larger scale, the pavilion (originally just a tent in the ancient Orient) became a far more substantial structure in 18th century France; in fact it could be called the garden building of the royals. Some were large enough to be used as guest houses, while others were said to have been used to accommodate a favoured mistress. Although these grand pavilions were built of masonry, later designs (including the park bandstand) were commonly made of wood.

On a more practical level, a range of utility buildings, designed for housing animals, storing tools and keeping fruit and other foodstuffs, became popular in Europe during the 19th century. One of the most interesting was the French *ferme orné*, essentially an 'ornamental farm'. In England these solid structures were used to disguise what might have been ugly, utilitarian buildings.

But probably the oldest garden building which was built in brick or masonry was the dovecote, designed for keeping pigeons and doves. The ancient Romans are believed to have invented this structure, designing rounded stone towers with nest holes and little shelves built into the walls from the ground all the way up to the top. In both France and early England, elaborate dovecotes were constructed from stone, while in colonial America, attractive brick dovecotes were a feature in some of the grander gardens. In South Africa, thickly plastered and whitewashed ones were found in the grounds of some of the early Cape Dutch manor houses.

Nowadays these bird houses are more commonly set on a single post and are frequently made of wood.

A charming traditional gazebo built alongside a brick garden wall provides shelter.

This unusual sunken greenhouse comprises brick walls with a glass and timber roof.

a section of the unit with doors. This can be used for items which may blow away or deteriorate if they get wet; firewood, on the other hand, may be stacked under the surface which forms the fire bed, even if it is partially open to the elements.

The materials chosen to front an outdoor cupboard or to cover a brick container will have a major effect on the design. Timber is the first choice, but it should be sealed or painted to improve its appearance as well as to increase its lifespan.

Bin shelters and similar structures are functional and they do hide objectionable items from view, but it is important to ensure that they look as though they belong and fit in with the design of the outdoor area in which they are located. If a brick wall adjacent to a storage unit has been rendered with mortar and then painted, it is advisable to use the same finish

on the bin shelter. If it is built next to a wooden fence, match the door of the storage unit to the timber used for the fence.

Although timber (or even wire) is probably more common for compost bins, brick is a suitable option. Since circulating air is essential for the waste vegetable and plant material to break down, it is best to use pierced screen blocks or to build the walls using bricks laid in a honeycomb pattern, leaving gaps between the ends of each brick. Ideally, a compost bin should have two or even three compartments so that as one heap decomposes, you can start the next one off.

Pergolas and gazebos
Pergolas and other overhead shelters (sometimes referred to as arbours), are common on patios, whether they are located alongside the house, in the garden, or beside an activity area

like a tennis court or swimming pool. Sometimes built against the wall of the house (which provides a support at one end or along one side), pergolas consist of upright pillars, poles or posts with lighter overhead beams and crosspieces. Some are topped with roofing (see pages 26–27), while others are left open or used as a support for climbing plants.

A variety of materials can be used for the uprights of a pergola, but masonry is undoubtedly one of the more popular options. The design should be in harmony with existing architectural influences and the proportions in keeping with the size of the property as well as existing garden features and other buildings on the property.

A well-designed carport may also feature brick pillars, but the roof is often more solid than that of a pergola.

Although most modern gazebos are probably built of wood or metal, brick is an option which may be considered for more solid side walls, even if these only extend halfway up the structure. When combined with brick pillars, a design of this type can be an unusual and attractive feature in the contemporary garden.

Play structures
Although the majority of play structures are built out of timber, there is nothing stopping you from building a playhouse from bricks and mortar. In fact this a perfect project to practise on for anyone who has the basic skills and who is planning to try their hand at some more challenging bricklaying, like a garden building or a boundary wall which incorporates planters.

Bricks may be used to build a simple structure like a sandpit for young children. It need be no larger than 1.5 m x 1.5 m and no more than three courses high. Positioned where it could later look attractive with shrubs and flowers in it, a sandpit may be used as such until your children tire of it and then easily converted into a planter.

It is essential to ensure that the sub-base of any sandpit will allow water to drain away naturally. If it does not, it will become a quagmire after heavy rain. It is also a good idea to cover a sandpit to prevent cats and dogs from fouling the sand.

Garden buildings
Few people today can afford the type of garden buildings which were created during the 16th–18th centuries in Europe and Britain as banqueting houses or secret hideaways. However, there are numerous quite simple garden structures which may be built from bricks, blocks and various other similar materials.

Tool sheds and outdoor workrooms built from brick will provide you with a permanent place to carry out menial activities or to undertake DIY projects which would make a mess elsewhere. Greenhouses and conservatories can also be built from brick, with glass panels or even a glass or polycarbonate roof allowing sunlight to enter.

Barns and animal shelters may also be built from bricks and mortar. In fact masonry is the ideal material for this type of building, particularly if it is to house horses, cows or other animals. Not only will it provide a solid, stable shelter, but it can be easily cleaned by hosing it down with water.

Although not particularly common nowadays, changing rooms can be useful beside a swimming pool on a large property. Little more than sheds, these structures can be planned to accommodate pool cleaning equipment, pumps, filters, chlorination units, as well as recreational items such as lilos and beach balls, and folding outdoor furniture.

There are various roofing possibilities for all of these buildings, which will provide adequate shelter from the elements. The most suitable types include sheeting in its many guises, thatch and tiles.

STYLE
There is no doubt that small buildings and other structures will contribute to the general style and character of your garden. If your house has a definite style, try to echo the look of it, and devise a scheme which will complement it rather than compete with it. For instance, a pretty, white cottage will benefit from features like a small, modern dovecote, an informal pond, arches and perhaps even a wishing well. A Victorian-style garden will demand a traditional gazebo for authenticity, while one in a Japanese style will gain character from natural stone seating. The larger English country garden can usually accommodate a range of structures, including a traditional pergola, perhaps in the style of Sir Edwin Lutyens. If your house is a clean-lined one built in facebrick, it is usually best to match the materials as well as the style.

A thatched shelter built with bricks and mortar is perfect for outdoor entertaining in most weather conditions.

MATERIAL OPTIONS

There is a surprisingly wide choice of materials for garden structures which are to be built in masonry. Both clay and concrete bricks are manufactured in a range of colours and finishes, and concrete blocks are available either hollow, pierced, or in the form of reconstructed or reconstituted stone. Some types of bricks or blocks are intended to be left as they are, while others should be rendered with mortar and then painted.

In some areas clay and/or mud adobe blocks are available, and many of the structures we have suggested may also be built with natural stone.

Clay and concrete bricks

Available as facebricks for rendering or plastering, these materials are a popular choice for garden masonry structures. There is a wide range of colours and textures to choose from, which means you are sure to find something that will suit any garden environment. Brick sizes are relatively standard, differing slightly from country to country. They are relatively small and therefore easy to handle, making them the perfect choice for the first-time builder.

Your choice of brick will depend largely on the style and character of the structure you are building. The most expensive option is clay facebrick (also called facing brick) which is strong and long-lasting in all weather conditions – an important consideration in areas which experience severe frost and snow or constant sea spray. You will find, though, that specifications differ, and where conditions are harsh, it is wise to check durability factors with your supplier or manufacturer.

Concrete facebricks are also available in a range of textures and colours, although these are not as natural as the hues of clay brick.

If you plan to render the surface of your structure, it makes sense to use non-face bricks (or non-facings).

These are much cheaper than facebricks, and are not intended to be left unprotected.

Concrete blocks

Standard blocks, manufactured in a reasonably wide range of sizes, are a cost-effective option. Not only are they cheaper than bricks (when compared per square metre), but these hollow units are also quicker to lay because of their size.

As ordinary concrete blocks are not particularly attractive, in most instances you will need to render (plaster) the finished surface. Another possibility is to camouflage the structure with a brick veneer, although this will involve additional work and will also increase costs because of the extra materials required.

Screen blocks

A range of attractive screen blocks with pierced patterns may be used within the garden. Commonly used for

Attractive facebricks have been used to build a characterful arched entrance and matching boundary wall.

both boundary and screen walls, these units allow both light and air to pass through the structure. Since they are laid in a stack bond, which is not particularly strong (see page 32), they are only suitable for certain applications, where intermediate piers help support them.

Pierced blocks could be used to construct a simple compost bin, provided the pattern of holes is not too open.

Reconstituted (reconstructed) stone blocks

Manufactured from concrete in imitation of stone, reconstituted stone blocks and smaller brick-like units are ideal for the full range of garden structures and buildings, as long as they will suit the style of your garden and existing structures. Colours and textures are chosen to blend with natural stonework, and sizes to correspond to the typical dimensions of cut stone.

An advantage of building with reconstituted stone rather than the genuine material is that these blocks are considerably easier to lay because of their regular shapes and sizes. Large jumper blocks, which are the height of two courses, are sometimes available in a variety of different sizes for authenticity.

Clay and mud blocks

Although clay blocks are fired in the same way as clay bricks, adobe blocks (or mud bricks) are manufactured in quite a different way, and are only available in some parts of the world.

Traditional adobe structures eventually deteriorate, but nowadays these blocks are stabilised with asphalt, cement or straw to prevent them from crumbling and decomposing. Larger than clay bricks (and even some clay blocks), adobe blocks are solid and heavy, and therefore relatively cumbersome to work with.

Stone

The craft of stone masonry is an ancient one which has been passed down through the ages in just about

A combination of stone and brick works well.

every country in the world. Whether you use cut or dressed stone or lay irregular rocks in a random pattern, the effects attained will add charm to any garden. Stone is suitable for many garden features, although it is considerably more difficult to lay than brick and block.

Various types of stone are found in different areas; your choice will depend on availability.

ROOFING POSSIBILITIES

Brick pergolas, gazebos, walkways and various garden buildings built with masonry units may incorporate simple roofs which offer some shelter from the sun, rain and wind. A shed or summerhouse will, of necessity, have a roof which provides a greater degree of protection than the average pergola.

It is not surprising that the type of roof chosen will depend largely on the degree of shelter you require from the elements. Awning material (shadecloth), for instance, will be quite adequate for a pergola which will provide shade, while a tool shed will demand something much more substantial. A gazebo traditionally incorporates a tiled or shingled roof while the covering chosen for a rustic summerhouse might be thatch, if this material is available.

As with all other materials, the type of roofing you choose must complement the materials used elsewhere. This does not mean you necessarily have

Sundial on a concrete slab set on stone.

to match the roof to your house, but any new material you introduce should blend well with it.

The supporting structure of the roof will depend on what it will cover and the load it will bear; however, specific structural elements are not considered in any detail here as more substantial buildings will require greater expertise than is necessary for the projects discussed in this book.

Plants

If you do not want to cover a pergola or similar overhead structure with roofing, plants should always be considered. You will find that a wide variety of climbers and creepers are suitable for this purpose. Not only will they make the structure look attractive, but flowering species will also add colour, and many types will give off a delightful fragrance as well. A pergola is an effective structure for supporting plants; if properly trained, they will soon form a charming, natural ceiling.

The type or types of plant you choose will depend on what is available at your local garden centre, but suitable species include honeysuckle and the various jasmines. Clematis, wisteria and vines will all lose their leaves in winter, but this allows the sun to filter into an area which might otherwise become cold, damp and unusable at certain times in the year. Of course, bear in mind that any climbing plants will take time to grow.

Awning material

Awning material is available in various guises and is a good choice for pergolas located on patios which require some shade. Although some types are water-resistant, most are not waterproof and will therefore not give any protection from the rain.

Most retractable awnings are made from canvas, which is available in many different colours, both plain and patterned (usually striped).

Shadecloth, made from a hardy acrylic material and sold in several parts of the world, is available in a variety of fashion colours as well as in green and black, the hues more commonly used for horticultural purposes. Various densities offer anything from 30% to 85% protection from the sun's rays. This material should be cut with a soldering iron to prevent it from fraying and should never be placed over timber that has been treated with creosote, as this will cause it to deteriorate.

Roofing felt

Bituminous roofing felt is a reasonably inexpensive option particularly suitable for sheds, carports and utility garden buildings. It is usually sold in rolls and nailed to plywood, hardboard, particle board, masonite or whatever other boarding has been used over the roof trusses or battens.

Although this material has a reasonably long lifespan, it may need to be resealed with a bituminous waterproofing compound from time to time. Odd holes, including those created by nails, may be sealed with bitumen paste or mastic.

Roof sheeting

A wide range of sheeting is suitable for the roofs of all kinds of garden buildings. Some types are available as flat sheets, but most are corrugated. All types are suitable for brick buildings with roofs that have a minimum pitch of 5-10° although cost will probably determine what you choose for a simple utility shed or animal shelter. If sheeting is used for a pitched roof, you will have to fix capping along the

A combination of reeds and plants form the roof of this simple, rendered pergola.

ridge; if it is used for a structure which abuts a building, you will need to seal the join with flashing to prevent rain and moisture from seeping through the gap. Remember too, that whatever kind of roof sheeting you are using, the sheets must overlap at the joins. Some will need to be predrilled prior to installation, although self-drilling roofing screws are usually sufficient.

One of the cheapest kinds of roof sheeting is fibreglass, which is suitable not only for a range of small garden buildings but also for open-sided structures like pergolas and carports. Lightweight and easy to handle, it is available in several different profiles and a range of translucent colours.

Polycarbonate, a smooth, synthetic material which looks like glass or perspex, is better suited to pergolas and conservatory-type extensions. It comes in flat or corrugated sheets, and is available in the same sheet sizes as fibreglass and metal.

Another lightweight, corrugated

variety of sheeting is Onduline (a trade name), which is manufactured in France from organic fibres which have been saturated in bitumen. Widely distributed, it is available in brown, black, bottle green, red and translucent, and is perfect for outbuildings and overhead structures which require a solid roof.

Both corrugated iron and aluminium sheeting (which is also used for some awnings) may be used, but the latter is a relatively expensive option, particularly for an outbuilding. Special tools are required to cut it, and because it is relatively 'soft' it is easily damaged. For this reason it is generally installed by professionals. On the other hand iron, which is available galvanised or colour-coated, is reasonably priced and particularly popular for carports.

Although heavy, fibrecement is another option which is usually relatively inexpensive. Also manufactured in a selection of profiles,

It requires sturdy roof trusses and carport beams, depending of course where it is to be used.

Tiles and shingles

Many traditional garden buildings constructed with bricks and mortar or stone had roofs which were finished in tile or with slates or shingles. Today garden buildings of all kinds are roofed with these materials, provided that they have a minimum pitch of 15–26°; generally the rougher the finish, the greater the pitch required.

Flat slate and clay tiles, as well as shingles (made from wood, asphalt, aluminium or glass fibre) or thicker wooden shingles are perfect choices for a gazebo roof.

Ordinary tiles, made from various materials including clay, fibrecement and reconstituted stone, may be used to cover outbuildings, summerhouses, sheds and simple pitched pergolas.

Thatch

Suitable for pitched pergolas and some garden buildings, thatch requires a minimum pitch of about 45°. A popular choice for open-sided summerhouses in some hot climates, as well as in many traditional designs, it is usually installed by a skilled craftsman. If you favour this material, you will need to ensure that the roof structure is made with wooden poles rather than sawn timber.

If natural thatch is not readily available in your area, consider the option of acrylic thatch.

Reeds, bamboo and timber

Attached to the crossbeams of a pergola, these natural materials will produce attractive dappled shadows, and provide shade as well as some shelter from the wind and light rain. Bamboo and reeds may also be used as a ceiling, within a building (possibly a summerhouse or a shelter for entertaining) or on a patio which has a more substantial roof.

Timber is the most common of these three materials, probably because it is available everywhere. Laths may be arranged across the beams in a regular row, as closely or widely spaced as you wish. Obviously the smaller the gaps between the lengths of timber, the more shade and shelter you will have. If the laths are too close, this can make an enclosed area look dark and gloomy. As an alternative to straight laths, a pergola may be topped with latticework, which you can make yourself or buy ready made.

Where reeds and bamboo are available, these materials make charming patio roofs. If they are not readily available commercially, there may be a supplier in your area that has access to the material in the field. If you cannot track anyone down, try advertising in the classified section of your local newspaper.

In some areas you can buy bamboo in woven rolls, ready for installation. If you can't find these, string the stalks together to form your own panels or attach them directly to the pergola beams. Ideally you should use green material that has not yet dried out; this prevents unnecessary splitting and ensures that the lengths fit neatly side by side. You can either tie the lengths in place, or predrill them before nailing them to the timber. Set the reeds with thick and thin ends alternating to ensure an even finish.

LIGHTING

Although not every garden is illuminated at night, some form of exterior lighting is essential, not only for safety, but for security as well. It is dangerous if you cannot see where you are going, and if you cannot detect intruders.

It makes sense to install lighting in most garden buildings, especially if you want to make use of them in the evenings. If they are situated some distance from the house, you may require additional wiring. You can probably lay low-voltage cables and fix fittings yourself, but the actual mains connection should be installed by a registered electrician.

Patios should also be illuminated, and those which are attached to the house often make use of existing fittings. You will need good general lighting, rather than spotlights or uplighters. Where new fittings are installed, these must be suitable for outdoor use – most lighting shops have a good selection of sealed units from which to choose.

Features in the garden are usually lit up at night for decorative purposes only. Uplighters are ideal for highlighting foliage, and popular low voltage systems are perfect for this.

An open brick building has a thatched roof installed by a skilled craftsman.

A thorough knowledge and understanding of basic building principles is essential for anyone tackling an outdoor project in brick. Not only is it essential to know the correct techniques for laying bricks and ensuring they are properly bonded, but it is also important that all structures are square, level and plumb.

An experienced bricklayer knows the value of using the correct tools and appreciates the importance of working with the right concrete and mortar mixes. If your structure is to look professional, it is vital that you familiarise yourself with these elements. It is also useful to have some basic knowledge of quantifying materials, so that you can cost the project reasonably accurately and avoid the unnecessary wastage which is so often incurred when ordering is based on guesswork.

THE ESSENTIAL TOOLKIT

Although certain very specific tools are required for bricklaying, the essential toolkit is not extensive. All items are available at builders' stockists, hardware stores and major do-it-yourself outlets.

In addition to those listed below, you will need a spade to excavate the earth, possibly a shovel to mix concrete and mortar (although you can also use a spade), a pick if the ground is hard or stony, and a wheelbarrow to transport bricks, mixed materials and excess soil to and from the excavation.

If you are planning to incorporate timber seat tops or wooden lids and cupboard doors in your brick structure, you will also need a basic carpentry kit, with saws, a drill, screwdrivers and a hammer. A combination square (sometimes referred to as a carpenter's square) is also useful.

Compactors

A punner, or ramming tool, is handy for compacting the earth or fill beneath footings. It can be made by filling an empty 5 litre paint can with concrete and inserting a pole or length of timber as a handle. The flat end of a fairly heavy round pole may be used instead, but if you need to compact a large area, it is advisable to hire a compacting machine.

Straightedge

Invaluable for extending the usefulness of a spirit level over large areas, a straightedge may be made of metal or timber. If wood is chosen, make certain it is not warped or bowed. A straightedge may also be used for compacting and smoothing concrete, for levelling mortar on a rendered surface, and as a gauge rod.

Tape measure

A good quality, retractable steel tape is the builder's best friend, as it is used from the setting-out stage, until completion of the project.

Gauge rod

An invaluable aid for keeping brick and block courses regular, a gauge rod is simply a flat, straight-edged length of timber or metal which is marked off according to the height of each course, at intervals equal to one brick or block plus a mortar joint. Some professionals mark their spirit level in the appropriate gauges, so they do not have to use two tools during bricklaying. The dimensions chosen will depend on the size of the masonry unit you are using as well as the thickness of the mortar joints. A foolproof method is to lay the first two courses and then to use this to guide you when marking it off.

Builder's square

One of the tools no bricklayer should be without, a builder's square is made of steel and is marked off like a ruler.

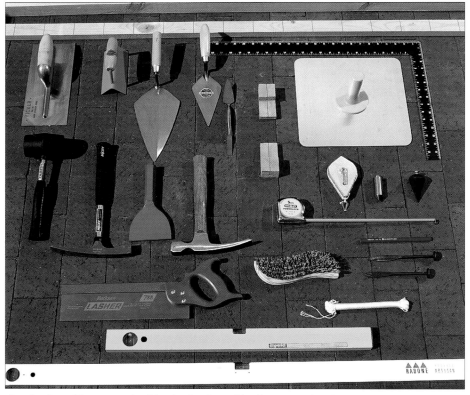

A selection of items required for the basic toolkit of anyone planning to tackle bricklaying.

A builder's square is an essential tool to ensure that all corners are at 90˚.

Considerably larger than a mathematical set square, it performs a similar function, enabling you to check that all corners are at 90˚. When setting out a structure, you may find that a builder's square is not big enough; if so, you can make a bigger one out of timber, using the 3:4:5 method (see below and page 37). Make sure that the angle you create is correct or your structure will not be square.

Spirit level
An indispensable tool, a spirit level is used at every stage of the building process to ensure that foundations and both horizontal and vertical brick surfaces are level and plumb. Made of metal, this tool incorporates both a horizontal and a vertical vial; if the bubble is in the centre, the surface is level. When laying out a drainage slope, you can put a block of wood under one end of the level to achieve the required slope (see below). A line level, which is basically a vial without a straight-edged metal casing, may be strung onto a builder's line and used as an additional aid. It cannot be used to check for plumb.

Line and pins or corner block
A builder's line (or string) is used with wooden or metal pegs to set out the foundations for brick structures. Not only is string cheaper, but it is easier to see than a builder's line.

When laying bricks, builder's line is strung along the upper level of the course to be laid. It may be used in conjunction with metal pins, or with corner blocks (see page 31). Alternatively, you can simply wind the line around a brick to secure it.

Trowels, mortarboards and floats
A standard bricklaying trowel is essential for laying the bricks, while a rectangular plasterer's trowel is used when rendering walls. Although not vital, corner trowels are a useful addition to the toolkit. Shaped to fit either outside or inside corners, they simplify the task of neatening the vertical edges of a rendered structure. A mortarboard or screedboard (or hawk) is useful, but certainly not high on the list of priorities for the essential toolkit. Many professionals use this tool to hold small quantities of mortar while they lay the bricks or render the surface. When working at ground level, you can simply dip into the wheelbarrow; alternatively use a flat piece of metal or board.

If the surface is to be rendered, you will need to purchase a wooden float to smooth the mortar once it has been laid on. A steel float is not generally used for external walls.

Pointing and jointing tools
Various pointing and jointing tools are used to place mortar in the joints and

A straight-edged piece of timber, marked off to indicate brick courses, is used as a gauge rod.

to rake it out, respectively. A pointing trowel (which looks like a small-scale bricklayer's trowel) is normally used to fill in small holes in the mortar. If you butter the ends of the bricks properly as you work, you should be able to manage without one.

While a narrow trowel or special jointer may be used to finish both vertical and horizontal joints, a piece of metal, cut to form a square tip, is quite adequate. Traditionally joints were finished in various ways; they could be either concave, flush, recessed to a square finish, or even jointed so that the mortar stuck out slightly. But there is an art to these techniques, and the DIY builder need do no more than rake out the excess mortar to neaten the joint.

A float is used to screed a concrete slab.

Brick-cutting tools

There are several options for cutting bricks. Probably the simplest is to use a brick hammer, which has a chisel end for this purpose, although it does not always cut neatly, especially if you are not adept at handling it. A bolster or broad chisel may be used instead. Place the brick on the ground (preferably on a bed of sand) and score the surface to mark the required cutting line; place the chisel blade on the line and knock firmly with a hefty club hammer. For very hard bricks, an electrically powered angle grinder is a boon.

Block splitters and masonry saws may be used for cutting larger concrete blocks; they may be hired if you do not want to buy one.

Rubber mallet

The best tool for knocking paving bricks level, this rubber-headed hammer is also useful for tapping stubborn bricks into place.

Saws

Although not strictly part of the bricklayer's toolkit, a saw is essential if you are cutting timber to make corner blocks, straightedges and so on.

BUILDING PRINCIPLES

Any well-built brick structure will be square, level and plumb. The exceptions, of course, are curved walls and circular structures, in which case there will obviously be no need to aim for right-angled corners.

Square

It stands to reason that any rectangular (or square) structure must have right-angled corners. If it does not, you will end up with crooked walls and a structure which is skew. For this reason it is essential not only to set out the structure correctly (see below and page 37) but also to use a builder's square to check the corners regularly as brickwork progresses. Never rely on your own judgement. Your workmanship may look absolutely square to you, but even the slightest inaccuracies can make a difference.

Level and plumb

Horizontal surfaces must be level, and vertical surfaces plumb. To ensure that they are, it is essential to check them at every stage. Make sure that the excavation is level, the foundation slab is absolutely flat, and the brickwork is even. It is vital not to rely on guesswork, otherwise you will have problems and may find yourself having to demolish what you have built.

The most common, and certainly the most versatile, tool used for this purpose is a spirit level. It will enable you to check both horizontal and vertical surfaces, at all stages and in all positions. For instance, as brickwork progresses, you can use a spirit level to check the upper surface of the bricks. By setting it on a straight-

A brickhammer is used to halve a brick.

An angle grinder is useful for cutting bricks.

A bolster and club hammer used together.

edged length of timber, you can check that two corners are at the same height. You can also check the vertical sides of the bricks, to ensure that the wall of brickwork is rising square and true, and you can use it on the diagonal to make sure the vertical surface is even.

A builder's line can also be used to keep brick courses level. Hooked onto the corner of the brickwork with

A spirit level is an essential tool to ensure that brickwork is level and plumb.

corner block, or attached by sticking special pins into the mortar, it creates a constant guide at whichever level you set it at. On a large expanse of wall, it may be used in conjunction with a line level.

Although corner blocks are sometimes available commercially, they are easily and quickly made with offcuts of wood. You will need two blocks of wood approximately 100 mm x 50 mm x 50 mm. Cut a section out of each to form a chunky L-shape, and then saw half-way through the foot of the L to create a slot which will hold the line in place. Wind the line around the base of the foot and draw it through the slot. The block is then hooked onto the corner of the brickwork at the correct height, and the line stretched to the opposite corner where it is attached to a second corner block.

Although a plumb bob may be used to check vertical surfaces at corners, relatively few people bother with this tool. It is really only useful on a large expanse of wall, for instance a multi-storey building.

Bonding

It is vital that all bricks are properly bonded so that the walls of the structure are strong and form a solid mass. This ensures that the load is distributed laterally, along the entire length of the wall. If the brickwork is not bonded, the vertical joints (or perpends) will be in a straight line and the load will not be distributed at all.

There are various ways of bonding brickwork, and several different patterns which have been used for centuries. The simplest, which is also the most common, is known as stretcher (or running) bond.

Stretcher bond brickwork is achieved by laying bricks so that they overlap those in the course below by half. Not only is the result attractive, but it is incredibly strong as well. It is also the only structurally sound bond which can be used to build a half-brick wall (comprising a single skin of brickwork), and the most economical when a cavity wall (with two rows of parallel brickwork) is constructed. Furthermore, it is the obvious choice when building a wall which is to be rendered, since there is little point in creating a plethora of patterns which will not be visible. When a one-brick wall is built in facebrick, any of the other options may be used, as you will find that the patterns created are quite different to stretcher bond.

English bond, believed to be the strongest of all bonds, is created by laying alternate courses of headers and stretchers. A course of headers is laid across a double skin of brickwork, where each brick is placed at right angles to the main run of bricks, exposing just the end, or header, on the outer wall.

English garden wall bond is a variation of ordinary English bond and

Corner blocks, easily made from blocks of wood, help keep brick courses straight.

consists of a header course followed by three to five stretcher courses.

Flemish bond consists of alternating headers and pairs of stretchers in the same course. The headers in the second course are centred over the stretchers of the first, and *vice versa*.

Flemish garden wall bond consists of a header followed by two or three pairs of stretchers in the same course.

MATERIALS

The basic ingredients of all masonry work are the same. You will need bricks, blocks or stone, as well as mortar made with cement, sand and water (and sometimes lime or plasticiser to bind the units together). You will also need concrete foundations or footings, made with cement, sand, a coarse aggregate and water. Metal reinforcement may be required in the foundations or between the brickwork. Timber may be required for seating, storage compartments and cupboards, as well as for formwork when pouring or casting concrete slabs.

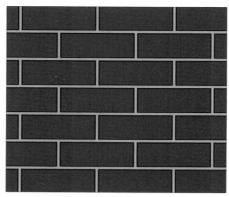

Stretcher bond is a common option.

English bond, probably the strongest bond.

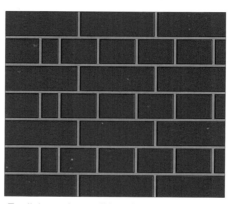

English garden wall bond.

Flemish bond has headers and stretchers.

A single or half-brick wall constructed using a stretcher bond pattern.

Bricks and blocks

Made from clay, concrete or calcium silicate, bricks and blocks are available in a range of reasonably standard sizes, depending on where they are made. Your choice will depend largely on what kind of structure you are building and whether it is to be rendered and painted or left with the face of the brick showing.

Although reconstituted (reconstructed) stone blocks are solid, many other concrete blocks are hollow. Bricks, on the other hand, may have an indent (or frog) in one face, or they may have two or three holes in them. Paving bricks are generally solid and flat. Both frogs and holes will aid bonding, and these characteristics are formed as a result of different methods of manufacture – indented bricks are moulded, while the holes are caused by a more modern process of extrusion.

In addition to standard bricks and blocks, bricks shaped in various ways are available for finishing walls and other brickwork. Pavers, of course, may be used to top a table or the working surface of a barbecue or outdoor bar structure, while bullnosed bricks (which are rounded along one side or at one end) may be used to finish ends neatly. They are also useful for laying around ponds and other decorative features. Various coping (or capping) bricks are also available.

The quality of bricks does vary. For instance, those manufactured for general building work that is to be rendered may deteriorate if they are not coated with mortar. You will also find that there is some variation in the size and finish of different facebricks. Ask your supplier for information regarding those available in your area.

Apart from the bricks chosen to build your structure, you may decide to use firebricks on the cooking surface of a barbecue and tough engineering or exposure-grade bricks where walls are likely to be exposed to constant damp. If necessary, seek professional advice.

Bricks are available in a variety of shapes and sizes for both paving and construction work.

Cement

Ordinary Portland cement, suitable for most concrete and mortar work, is used internationally. Sold in sealed 50 kg (and sometimes 25 kg or 40 kg) pockets or bags, it should be stored in a waterproof environment, preferably stacked above the ground and covered with plastic sheeting. If cement gets wet, it will become lumpy and unusable. Unless you are involved in a major building project, do not buy more cement than you can use within a maximum of three months.

Sand

Sold in volume or in open bags (usually containing about 25 kg or 50 kg), sand must be of a good quality and suitable for building. The best sands are evenly graded, containing particles of various sizes. Sand that does not contain sufficient fine material ('fines') will tend to produce a weak, porous surface layer if it is used for concrete. If sand is too fine, mortar will tend to rise to the surface of the concrete. If the particles are mostly the same size, the concrete will be difficult to work with.

In areas where sand is graded as 'soft' and 'sharp', you should use the soft sand for bricklaying and the coarser sharp sand for making concrete. Where plaster sand is available, this contains lime and is suitable for mortar to be used for both bricklaying and rendering. Otherwise it is usually best to add your own lime or plasticiser (see page 34).

Concrete blocks are laid with mortar in the same way as clay bricks.

For very large jobs it is advisable to order ready-mixed concrete, delivered in a truck.

Premixed and ready-mixed concrete

Although premixed materials, packaged dry in bags, are suitable only for very small jobs, ready-mixed concrete, delivered by volume in special trucks, is only appropriate for larger projects . You will, however, be assured of the exact strength of the concrete as the mixes are determined scientifically.

Lime

Available at the same outlets that supply cement, loosely bagged sand and aggregate, hydrated builder's lime improves the cohesiveness and water-retention qualities of fresh mortar. Available in 25 kg bags or pockets, it is a particularly useful additive if the sand is coarse or lacks very fine particles. Adding lime is also a good precaution to take against the mortar cracking.

Agricultural lime, road lime and quicklime (calcium oxide) are not suitable for brickwork.

Although the source of sand is not necessarily a foolproof guide, you will find that river sand is generally clean, and it often contains hard, rounded particles which increase the workability of concrete.

A disadvantage is that the fine particles have sometimes been washed out by the river water. Beach sand tends to be poorly graded, and it usually contains shell particles and salt. If it has been properly washed and graded by the supplier, it may be suitable for building use. Fine, wind-blown sands from desert areas and mine-dump sand (which is also too fine and uniform in particle size) should be avoided. You may find a blended sand which contains some clay, making the mortar easier to work.

Aggregate (crushed stone)

The coarse aggregate which is used to give bulk to concrete may be in the form of gravel, natural pebbles or crushed stone. Although its properties have less effect on the characteristics of the concrete than do the properties of the sand used, aggregate is usually screened to what is known as single sizes. The most popular size for DIY projects is 19 mm (or 20 mm) aggregate. A smaller 13.2 mm stone is easier to work with, but you will need to add more cement to the mixture.

Like sand, aggregate is sold in bags or by volume from builders' suppliers or transport companies.

Plasticiser

Plasticiser can be added to mortar to make it more workable, although it has no bonding function. Usually 50 ml of the liquid is added to every 50 kg of cement, but check the manufacturer's instructions beforehand.

Small quantities of concrete may be mixed on site in a wheelbarrow.

Water

A safe rule of thumb when mixing both concrete and mortar is to use only water which is good enough to drink. If sea water is used, you will find that white powdery deposits tend to form on the surface. If the water is contaminated in any way, with chemicals, for instance, this could have an adverse effect on the cement.

Reinforcing

It is unlikely that you will have to reinforce the concrete footings of a garden structure. If you do, you will probably be acting on the advice and specifications of an engineer. Light mesh or a grid of steel rods may be required in the foundation trench, or you may have to set vertical steel bars into the concrete. These will then be built into the wall or pillars.

The most common form of reinforcing incorporated into brickwork itself is a wire mesh available in rolls which is laid over the horizontal plane of every fourth or fifth course. This material is particularly effective for reinforcing the upper surface of small openings left in walls, for example over storage compartments. It is not a substitute for a lintel, though.

Timber

Any wood used for an outdoor project must be sound and durable. Generally, hardwood (from broadleafed tree species) is preferable. However some

Various types of timber are suitable for garden projects.

softwoods (from conifers and pines) are very suitable. In areas where it is available, redwood is a favourite for use in the garden.

Whatever your choice, make sure that the timber has been properly processed or pressure-treated with preservatives, preferably at the sawmill. Some types of timber (in particular teak and balau) will weather well in the open air, but most require some kind of weatherproof sealant to ensure that they will be able to withstand the elements over an extended period of time.

QUANTIFYING AND COSTING

The quantity of materials required will have a direct bearing on the cost of any structure. Of course, if you choose to build one of the designs on pages 52–61, you can simply take the list of materials and work out what these items will cost you. Otherwise you will have to do some mathematical calculations first.

The easiest way to cost the materials required to build a structure is to work out exactly how many bricks will be needed, just as we have done on the Plans pages. Once you know this, you

Hoop-iron reinforcing, set in a footing, will help strengthen a pillar.

Steel reinforcing is laid in the foundation trench of a substantial wall.

can establish how much cement, sand and lime is needed for the mortar. It is a simple matter to determine the materials required for the footings and foundations, provided you have accurate dimensions.

Foundations and footings

The quantities and proportions of the cement, sand and aggregate required to make concrete for footings is dependent on the type of structure you are building. The larger it is, in terms of both area and height, the bigger the footings will have to be, and the stronger the concrete mix should be. However, low-strength concrete is quite adequate for the footings of the simple structures featured here. If you are working with 19 mm aggregate, the recommended proportions of cement, sand and crushed stone for hand compaction are 1:4:4. In areas where a good quality gravel is available, the preferred ratio is 1:3:6. If a stronger mix is required, alter these ratios to 1:3:3 (with crushed stone) or 1:2:3 (with gravel).

Local building regulations and codes specify minimum specifications for footings, including the necessary depth below the frostline where relevant. If you are at all uncertain, check these before you start building. As a guide, smaller structures may be built on footings which are between 100 mm and 150 mm thick; higher, more substantial walls will require a footing of at least 200 mm.

Once you have determined the dimensions relevant to your project, work out the volume of concrete required by multiplying the length x width x thickness or height. If you are using a 1:4:4 mix, you will need 4½–5 bags (225–250 kg) of cement for every cubic metre; for a 1:2:3 mix you will need eight bags (or 400 kg) for each cubic metre. Once you know how much cement is required, you can calculate how much sand and aggregate is needed.

Bricks and blocks

Usually the quickest way to work out brick quantities is to work out the total wall area of whatever you are building. For every square metre of half-brick wall you will need 50–55 bricks (depending on their size); for a one-brick wall you will need to double that number. To work out the number of blocks required, divide the wall area by the area of the side of one block.

When building smaller features, you can also draw the design to scale and establish how many bricks there will be in the first course of each section or side of the structure. Determine the height of the structure and divide this by the height of your bricks plus a mortar joint; this will give you the number of courses required for the vertical face. Repeat this process for every wall face in the design.

Mortar

When mixing mortar for bricklaying in the ratio 1:4 cement to sand, you can count on using 50 kg of cement for every 200 bricks laid in a half-brick wall, and the same amount for every 150 laid in a one-brick wall. Mortar works out at about 1 cubic metre per 1 000 bricks. When using larger blocks, the quantities vary; the larger the block, the less cement you will need per square metre. You will need 50 kg cement to lay a hundred 390 mm x 190 mm x 190 mm blocks, and the same amount of cement to lay about fifty 190 mm x 90 mm x 90 mm blocks. If you are planning to add lime, add 25 kg for every 50 kg of cement.

SETTING OUT

It is absolutely essential to set out the position of any structure correctly. Some helpful pointers are illustrated on page 40, including the useful 3:4:5 method of checking that corners are all kept at 90°. While a builder's square is a reliable guide, it is surprisingly easy to make a mistake and very useful to double-check the layout using this method. Another way to check that the layout is square is to measure diagonally between opposite corners. If you have set out the structure correctly, the two measurements will be the same.

If a structure is to be built on a patio where a slight drainage slope is required, you can set this out with a spirit level, one end of which should be set on a small block of wood. The

For your project to run smoothly, it is essential to plan the job and quantify materials carefully.

Use a straightedge to scrape and smooth wet concrete.
Concrete must set thoroughly before bricklaying or paving starts.

height of the block of wood will depend on the slope required. For a 1:50 slope, which is the minimum requirement, a 40 mm thick block placed under a 2 m long straightedge will do the trick. Place a spirit level on the straightedge, and position the block under one end of the timber. Then mark the slope with pegs.

If you want to level a slope, the simplest method is with a water level. Consisting simply of a length of transparent tubing (or garden hose with a piece of clear tubing pushed into either end), this homemade tool works on the principle that water finds its own level. Tie one end to a stake and knock this into the ground at the highest point or get a partner to hold it in place. Fill the tube with water before attaching it to a second stake, which should be positioned at the lowest point. Mark off the water level on both stakes, then measure the distance between this mark and the ground at the lowest stake. Then dig out the earth at the first stake to the same depth.

BUILDING TECHNIQUES
The building techniques required for outdoor brick structures are illustrated in detail on pages 40–51. Once you have familiarised yourself with them and had some practice, you will find that they really are not difficult at all.

Working with concrete
Although the principles of mixing concrete are simple, this can be backbreaking work, especially if you decide to mix by hand yourself. If there is a reasonable quantity of concrete to be used, it is usually advisable to hire a concrete mixer. You will, in any case, have to mix in batches, measuring out each one carefully. Use the same container (a large builder's bucket or a clean 25 litre drum) for measuring all the materials.

Mixing
If you are mixing by hand, work on a hard, clean surface. Never mix directly on the ground as soil can contaminate the concrete and moisture will be absorbed from the mixture. If you mix on asphalt or paving of any sort, hose the area down immediately to prevent the concrete from drying and staining the surface.

First combine the sand and cement until you get a uniform colour, then make a small crater in the centre and add water gradually, shovelling the dry materials into the centre at the same time. Take care not to add too much water, or you will wash the cement and sand from the heap. When the mix is soft and smooth, rather like thin porridge, you can add the crushed stone or gravel. Some builders prefer to mix all the dry materials first.

When using a concrete mixer, load the coarse aggregate first with a little bit of water and run the machine for a few minutes. This prevents the mix from building up on the blades. Add the sand next, and then the cement.

Placing
It is good building practice to dampen the foundation trench before placing or pouring the concrete, in order to prevent absorption of water from the mix into the soil. Pour the concrete out of a wheelbarrow, or shovel it into the trench. Tamp it down with the back of a spade or shovel, then use a straightedge to compact and level it. Start with a chopping motion and then use a sawing movement to finish. Stop when water starts to come to the surface.

Setting and curing
Concrete footings must be left to set, at least overnight, but preferably for several days before building on them. In cold weather, they should be protected from frost by covering them with sacking or plastic. In very hot weather, it is advisable to sprinkle or spray a little water on the surface from time to time to keep it moist.

The hardening of the concrete is the result of a chemical reaction between the cement and water. Although it continues to cure over a period of

A corner block is in place to ensure that bricks are laid correctly.

concrete is clean and has not accumulated sand and garden debris. Use the trowel to place a sausage of mortar on the foundation and make furrows in it with the pointed tip. Then slide the first brick into position. Now butter the end of your second brick, and slide this into place.

If you watch the professionals at work, you will see that they build up the corners of a wall first, stepping the brickwork back by half a brick at each course. This is known as racking back and it helps ensure that the structure is kept square. Use a spirit level (set on a straight-edged length of timber if it is too short) to check that opposite corners are level. Then string a builder's line between the two corners as a guide to laying the bricks in between. Use a gauge rod to check that each course is equal in height.

years, it gains most of its strength in the first 28 days.

Bricklaying

For anyone planning to do their own bricklaying, the most important tool you will have to learn to use is a bricklayer's trowel. Once you have mastered the technique of buttering the ends and sides of bricks with the trowel, you will be well on your way. The other vital aspect is to ensure that each and every brick you lay is level and plumb.

A spirit level will enable you to do this; just make certain that the bubble in the vial is always centred.

The mortar for bricklaying is mixed in exactly the same way as concrete, except that aggregate is not added. If lime is used, add this with the cement and sand.

Once you know which bond you are going to use (see pages 31–32), you can get started. The first course is laid on mortar set on the concrete foundation. Make sure that the

Rendering

If you are not using facebricks, you will probably want to render the surface once the brickwork is complete. Mortar is used, usually mixed in the same ratio as the bricklaying mortar so that the two are compatible. To make mortar more pliable, plasticiser or lime is usually added to the mixture. The

Butter mortar onto one end of the brick before putting it in place.

A metal pointing tool is used to scrape out the joints of brickwork.

addition of a bonding agent will also help the mortar stick to the surface.

If the brick surface absorbs too much water from the fresh render, the mortar will be weakened; spray some water evenly onto the brickwork the day before you are going to start work. If it has been raining, allow the walls to become surface-dry before applying the mortar. Remember that cracking is more likely if the mortar is applied in hot sun or strong wind conditions.

Once the mixture is ready, apply it to the surface using a rectangular plasterer's trowel; press it down firmly to ensure good adhesion. It needs to set for about an hour before you can scrape the surface with a straightedge or a screed board. Once you have a reasonably level surface, smooth it out further with a wooden float to get a really smooth finish.

Mortar used to render walls must not be allowed to dry out too quickly, otherwise it will not cure properly and it may crack. To prevent this, dampen the surface by hosing with a gentle spray several times a day over a two- or three-day period. It is important to ensure that the spray is really fine, otherwise it could damage the finish.

Paved surfaces

If work tops and garden tables are to be paved, you will usually lay the

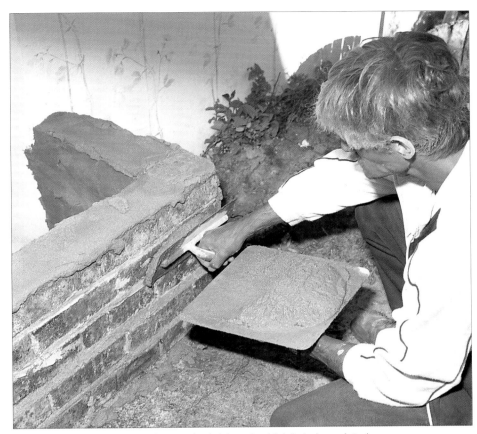

A normal mortar mix is used to render brickwork which is to be painted.

pavers in mortar in exactly the same way as any other bricks or blocks. On the other hand, when paving the fire bed of a barbecue structure, it is best to lay the pavers on sand, and to butt them up against one another

in order to form a solid base for the fire. Remember that clay bricks are fired at very high temperatures and will not be damaged by the fire; however, mortar or plain concrete base will tend to crack.

USEFUL TERMS

Aggregate Although sand is the fine aggregate added to both mortar and concrete, this term is also used to described the coarse aggregate added to concrete. This may be gravel or crushed stone, depending on what is available. In Britain, all-in aggregate (or hoggin) is a mixture of sand and gravel which is mixed with cement to make concrete. In South Africa, all-in aggregate is an inferior material which should be avoided.
Bond The arrangement of bricks to ensure that they overlap and therefore bind together to form a solid, stable mass. Various patterns may be formed, some of which, if laid in facebrick, can create a decorative effect.

Buttering Method used to apply mortar to the ends or sides of bricks during the bricklaying process.
Course A complete row of laid bricks. Several courses form a wall or part of another brick structure.
Excavation The foundation trench.
Footing Projecting concrete course at the foot of a wall, pillar or pier.
Foundation The concrete base on which brickwork rests.
Frog Indented side of a brick.
Jointing Method used to finish off and neaten the joints in brickwork when facebricks have been used.
Lap The amount a brick overlaps the bricks in the course below.

Header The short end of a brick. A header course features the end of the brick on the outside of the wall.
Perpend The vertical joints in brickwork.
Pointing The process of filling in joints with mortar.
Racking back Method of building up the brickwork at the corners and ends of walls.
Reinforcing Metal mesh or rods built into concrete and brickwork to strengthen it.
Stretcher The long side or face of a brick; hence stretcher bond (running bond). A stretcher course features the long side of the brick on the outside of the wall.
Weep holes Unmortared joints left in the base of walls or planters for drainage.

STEP-BY-STEP BUILDING METHODS

In the following pages, important building principles and basic bricklaying techniques are outlined, along with a description of the materials and tools you will need to build a brick structure in your garden. These instructions show step-by-step how to employ the various skills, starting with a section which illustrates clearly how to set out any project. To make the building process more realistic, step-by-step photographs show several specific brick features being built.

One series of pictures follows construction of a simple barbecue unit which incorporates a very basic storage area.

The second shows how seating, tables, planters and a storage box are assembled. These structures are not presented as projects, and no materials lists are given. Instead, the focus is on the procedures followed and techniques used. Once you have mastered them, you should be able to tackle any outdoor brick project.

You will see how the principles previously explained are put into practice; how single and double walls are built, corners constructed and pillars incorporated into a design. You will also see how various tools are used. Shuttering is used to create a working surface alongside the fire bed of the barbecue, and the same project also demonstrates how to create an opening in any brick structure. Weep holes are left in the planters, illustrating a simple drainage method.

BUILDING METHODS: SETTING OUT

The first step in any outdoor building project is to set out the site correctly. You will need to decide exactly where the structure is to be located, according to the dimensions and layout of your plan, and then you will have to mark it out, clearly showing where foundation trenches must be dug. The foundations are always slightly larger than the structure itself, an important point to remember when setting out.

One of the advantages of building smaller garden features is that, because of their size, it is usually easy to double-check the layout. A good way to do this is to lay out loose bricks to check the area to be excavated and ensure that the design will fit the area intended for construction.

If there is a problem, it is much easier to sort it out now than when the bricks have been mortared.

Most structures tackled by DIY builders are square or rectangular in shape, so all the angles where walls meet one another will be 90°. Occasionally a design may feature acute or obtuse angles or curved lines.

The simplest way to check that corners are square (or at 90°) is to use the 3:4:5 method. What this means is that the length of the shortest side of the triangle must be equal to three units of measurement, the adjacent short side must be four, and the line which joins the two ends must be five units in length. If the structure is large enough, these may

be units of 3 m, 4 m and 5 m respectively; a much smaller unit may be 300 mm, 400 mm and 500 mm units. Any other multiples will also work, for instance 600 mm, 800 mm and 1 m.

You can set out a circular structure by making a basic compass with pegs and string. Knock one peg into the central point, attach string to it, and then rotate the string, marking a ring of points around the circumference. The most important thing to remember is that the length of the string must equal the radius of your circle.

Once the layout has been pegged, mark the position of the foundations or footings with dry cement, lime, chalk or even ordinary cake flour; the latter is usually the cheapest option.

Use the 3:4:5 method to check for square.

Use a peg and string to lay out circles.

Check your layout with loose bricks.

BARBECUE

Anyone who wants to build a simple brick barbecue in the garden or on a patio will find these step-by-step instructions invaluable. It does not matter whether you want to copy the design, adapt it, or simply to use the various basic building skills which are illustrated; this helpful guide will enable you to create a special structure of which you can be proud.

Various elements are covered, from foundation to finishes. The aim is to give a broad indication of what is involved when building a structure which will be used for cooking and storage. The inclusion of a solid, paved working top will increase the versatility of the design.

The fire bed featured here is sunken, and surrounded by brickwork on three sides. This means there is no need to use shuttering or any other form of reinforcing to create the cooking surface. Instead, a basic brick box is constructed and filled with soil removed from the foundation trenches. This is then compacted, topped with sand and paved with clay bricks.

Since many barbecue designs feature a storage area for firewood, coal and other items below the cooking area, the step-by-step project

also includes instructions which will enable you to tackle this design variation. The upper surface of the storage area forms a table for preparing food which is to be cooked on the barbecue or for serving, and a similar surface may be built as the fire bed itself. In this event, the most important element is the shuttering which is provided to support the surface during construction.

If a chimney of some kind is to be built, shuttering will also be necessary to support the front wall. Although the central cavity will be left open, the essential principles are the same.

This particular barbecue design measures 1.85 m x 710 mm and is 950 mm above the ground. There is a generous fire surface with dimensions based on the average metal drum, so often cut in half lengthwise for use by the outdoor cook. A 920 mm x 600 mm grid will slot in and cover this area.

MATERIALS

Facebricks are used for building because they are a low-maintenance option for any structure which is to be used for cooking. Matching paving bricks are laid in the fire bed, forming the exposed working surface, and they

are also used to finish the inside of the storage compartment.

If you decide to follow the design exactly, you will need 270 facebricks and 58 matching pavers (not allowing for wastage).

The shuttering used here is permanent, but it is not intended to be seen after completion of the structure. For this reason, relatively thin 10 mm x 150 mm wide fibrecement boards are placed over the opening to cover it. Once the surface is paved, this material is not visible. Any other slim board (or even metal) may be used, but it should be weatherproof. Concrete cast *in situ* and concrete lintels are not suitable.

FOUNDATIONS

As this is not a heavy structure, a foundation of 100–150 mm is ample; use a 1:4:4 or 1:3:6 concrete mix, depending on soil conditions and the aggregate available in your area.

When laying out the structure (see facing page), make sure that the foundations are about 100 mm wider than the brickwork on all sides. If the structure is to be built alongside paving laid previously, the foundation may be flush with the existing bricks.

1 Decide where the barbecue structure is to be located and peg it out with string as described on page 40. Make sure that all the measurements are accurate, and use a steel builder's square to ensure that the corners are at right angles.

2 The area pegged out here is adjacent to existing paving and measures 2.05 m x 810 mm. You can remove the pegs and string before you dig the foundations, provided that you mark the perimeter of the proposed trench with chalk, cement or flour first.

3 If the area where you are building is lawned you may be able to use the grass elsewhere in the garden. Use the sharp end of a spade to cut into the turf, then dig out the sods neatly and carefully. Keep any excess soil on one side.

4 Bricks placed on edge are useful to indicate the upper level of your concrete. Place a spirit level across the bricks and check that the base of the trench is level. If you want a deeper foundation, use pegs, marked to the correct height.

5 Now mix concrete following the instructions given on page 37. Moisten the soil in the trench to prevent the water from the fresh mix from being absorbed into the ground. Transport the mixture in a wheelbarrow and tip it out into the trench.

6 The concrete should be level with the top of the bricks (or pegs). Level it off roughly with the back of your spade or shovel, and then neaten with a straight-edged piece of timber, using a sawing movement. Use a chopping motion to compact.

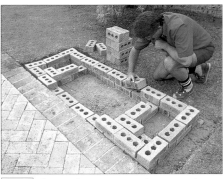

7 Once the concrete has set, lay out the bricks without mortar, positioning them correctly on the slab. Now is the time to make any minor alterations, for instance if you are not happy with the design or find that too many half bricks are needed.

8 Use a square to check that all four corners of the proposed structure are at 90°. Use a pencil or chalk to mark the position of the bricks on the concrete. Although you will have to recheck the angles later, this does help ensure accuracy.

9 Mix mortar in the ratio 1:4 (cement:sand), adding lime or plasticiser if required. Lay a sausage of mortar 10–15 mm thick where the first brick is to be laid. Use the tip of your trowel to make a jagged furrow along the centre of it.

10 Now you can bed the first brick in mortar. If it has obliterated the line you made on the concrete, use a steel square and the tip of the trowel to mark exactly where the brick should be positioned. Press the brick firmly into place and tap with the trowel.

11 It is essential that the first brick is flat and level, as you will use this surface to gauge the alignment of other bricks. Set the spirit level across the brick and check that the bubble in the vial is centred, tapping lightly with the handle of the trowel if it is not.

12 Check with the spirit level again, this time along the length of the brick. If the bubble in the vial is not centred, tap the brick gently with the trowel handle; alternatively, remove a little of the mortar from underneath the brick and check again.

13 Once the first brick is in place, you can butter one end of each onsecutive brick to be laid. Trowel on . wedge of mortar and spread it .cross the end. Then use the pointed p of your bricklaying trowel to make .rrows to aid bonding.

14 Put a little more mortar onto the slab, at right angles to the first brick you laid, and create a furrow in it as before. Slide the second brick into place, allowing the mortar on the end to form a joint. Push it firmly into the mortar and tap with the trowel handle.

15 You will not be able to tell whether or not it is perfectly level unless you use the correct tools. Place the spirit level across the upper surface of the two bricks and continue tapping gently with the trowel until the bubble is centred.

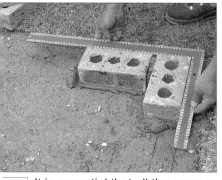

16 It is essential that all the corners of the structure are at right ngles. Even if you have followed all ne previous guidelines, use a steel uilder's square to check the angle gain now, before the mortar sets. hen lay your next brick.

17 You can lay the first course of the side wall, but do not lay the front wall until the first corner has been built up. This is the best way to ensure that the structure will be straight and square. Put mortar on the trowel and smooth it onto the bricks.

18 Lay the first brick of the second course at the corner, pushing it firmly into the furrowed mortar. Use the spirit level frequently to check that the upper surface is flat. As you work, make sure that the textured face of each brick is on the outside.

19 The surface which will form the outside walls must also be flat nd plumb. Do not forget to use the pirit level vertically to ensure that the nds of the bricks are properly aligned. ap the first brick in the second course utwards if it is not in line vertically.

20 Continue to build up the corner, checking all surfaces regularly. Even if both horizontal and vertical surfaces are flat, level and plumb, it pays to double-check across the diagonal. You can use a straightedge of any sort to do this.

21 The side walls are only three bricks long. Leave the middle brick out of the second course and lay a brick at the corner of the back wall. Check from corner to corner, across the full length of this section of wall before filling in to complete the course.

22 Scrape any excess mortar off the bricks with the trowel as you work. When using facebricks, it is much easier to keep the surface clean than to try to remove surplus mortar at a later stage. Do not waste what is scraped off; you can use it all.

23 Even though you are buttering the end of the bricks, you will find that there are a few gaps in the joints which need to be filled as you work. Lift a little of the mortar onto the trowel, and, using a chopping movement, point (or fill) these joints.

24 Now you can move to the opposite side of the structure and lay the first course at the corner. Once a few of the bricks are in place, string a line between the two corners, making certain that it is level with the upper surface of the bricks.

25 Then lay the course of bricks which will form the front wall of the barbecue and contain the fire bed. The line you have set up will enable you to make certain that it is absolutely straight; take care not to let any of the bricks touch it and push it out of place.

26 Continue building up the walls, using the bricks at each corner as a guide. If these are level with each other, you will find it easier to ensure that the course as a whole is level. It pays to be meticulous. Tap any uneven bricks with the trowel handle.

27 Once you have laid the first couple of courses at the front of the structure, lay the internal walls which will divide the cooking surface from the storage area. The position of these walls will depend on the design of your barbecue.

28 This design features a relatively wide fire bed, with storage space on one side only. A double brick wall on the other side provides a narrow serving area and will enable you to step the brickwork so that it provides a support for the grid.

29 Decide on the best position for the cooking grid. You will need to support it with metal (inserted into the mortar during bricklaying), or by stepping the brickwork. Lay the bricks at this level slightly off the edge of the wall below, so forming a narrow shelf.

30 Lay the bricks in the same way for the outside wall. This will result in a thicker mortar joint at this level, but it will not be obvious in the overall effect. The overlap should be equal on both sides, and just wide enough to support the grid.

31 Use a long spirit level to check that the bricks are level. If your spirit level is too short to span the gap, set it on a straight-edged piece of timber. Do not rely on your own judgement; if the bricks are not level the grid will wobble.

32 Now complete the brickwork, continually checking both the horizontal and vertical surfaces. Here the front wall is built up two courses for the storage area and seven for the fire bed. You may also create a second step for the grid if you wish.

33 Once most of the brickwork is complete, but before you lay the pavers on the upper surface, fill the central cavity with broken bricks, crushed stone or sand. You can also use the soil which was excavated from the foundation trench.

34 Use a punner or solid pole to compact the fill in layers and make certain there are no voids. This is especially important if you are using rubble which is not regular in shape and size. Hosing the fill gently with water also aids compaction.

35 Cut the shuttering to size. Here, 150 mm wide lengths of fibrecement are abutted to form a solid surface which will support the paving bricks. Brace the shuttering from underneath with timber. This can be removed once the mortar has set.

36 Matching pavers may now be laid in mortar, over the shuttering, to create a serving or working surface. Lay the first two at opposite corners and use the spirit level to check that they are level with one another before laying the balance.

37 Lay pavers over the entire upper surface. allowing those along the back wall to form a slight, decorative lip if you wish. Butter the ends of the bricks and use a trowel to fill in any open joints. Use a jointing tool to neaten the joints.

38 The pavers which are to form the fire bed are laid on sand rather than in mortar. Shovel a 25 mm layer of soft building sand over the fill, then smooth and level it with a straightedge. Abut the bricks and use a rubber mallet to level.

39 Use mortar to fill in around the edges of the pavers and keep them in place. Brush sand over the surface so that it fills the joints. Finally, use a piece of metal to rake out any excess mortar from the joints in the walls to give a nice, neat finish.

Brick features may be built as individual units or as part of a more elaborate plan. These step-by-step instructions will enable you to do either. You can copy the versatile design shown here, which incorporates ample seating, storage, built-in table tops and stepped planters, or construct any one of these features on its own. Alternatively, you can use the ideas and techniques demonstrated here to create your own design.

For those wanting to duplicate the design, the layout includes a 3.8 m long, 106 mm wide, half-brick wall which has three supporting 350 mm x 350 mm piers. This was included to shield a driveway from view and at the same time add privacy to the area. It is also used as the backrest to the bench which is set in front of it. The seat itself is constructed with six lengths of 70 mm wide timber which rest on three supporting piers, built to five courses above what will be the finished floor surface of the patio.

Tables are incorporated at both ends of the 2.3 m long bench; one measures 450 mm x 450 mm, while the other is only 450 mm x 220 mm, but quite adequate for drinks, plates and so on. Two planters, built to

different heights (one three courses high and the other five courses) are built at one end of the bench. The inside measurements of these are about 560 mm x 220 mm and 450 mm x 220 mm respectively. The storage box, which doubles as a second seating structure, is slightly wider than the bench (1.5 m x 700 mm), so that it can be used to store cushions and other bulky items. The lid, made with exterior plywood and planks, is hinged to an existing wall.

Since structures may be built on both strip and slab foundations (see page 36), both types are illustrated, along with an invaluable hint which will provide essential drainage in the base of a brick planter.

Most of the brickwork involves building single (or half-brick) walls, although construction of the central pier supporting the bench shows how the thicker one-brick wall is built.

MATERIALS

Although facebricks are used to construct all these features, part of the planter walls are rendered to blend with the exterior of the house. The tables and upper edge of the planters are topped with matching paving

bricks, providing a smooth and attractive surface. If you decide to copy the design, you will need about 300 facebricks and 13 pavers for the bench, storage box, tables and planters. An additional 300 will be required to build the 1.8 m high wall.

Various types of timber may be used for the seats, although you must be sure that it is suitable for outdoor use and will withstand weathering. Most types should be treated against infestation and sealed in some way (see page 35).

The interior walls of the planters are sealed with a bitumen-based product to prevent future discolouration caused by constant moisture.

FOUNDATIONS

Relatively small, 100–150 mm thick foundations are quite adequate for the smaller features. Foundations for the wall should be thicker (at least 200 mm thick); check whether your local authority or council has minimum requirements or guidelines for the area you live in.

When mixing the concrete, use a 1:4:4 or 1:3:6 concrete mix, depending on soil conditions and the aggregate available in your area.

1 Use a retractable steel tape and a builder's square to set out the foundation trenches as described on page 40. Make sure that they are about 100 mm wider on all sides than the structure itself. Peg out the area with long nails and string.

2 Before you begin to excavate the foundation trenches, mark the area pegged out with chalk, lime, cement or flour. Then remove the nails (or pegs) and string. This shows the layout of the screen wall and three supporting piers.

3 Dig the foundation trench for the wall and piers to a depth of at least 200 mm. Remove all vegetation and keep the ground surface as flat and even as you can, as this will enable you to cast an even slab to support the brickwork.

4 Mark out and dig the rest of the trenches to a depth of 150 mm. Strip foundations may be laid for the storage box structure, rather than throwing a solid slab. Make sure these are at least 100–200 mm wider than the walls will be.

5 Use a straightedge set on bricks, together with a spirit level, to determine where the upper surface of the concrete will be. The bricks are then left in position, as a permanent and failsafe guide.There is no need to remove them from the trench.

6 Once all the trenches have been dug and levelled, mix concrete as described on page 37 and transport it in a wheelbarrow. To prevent water from being drawn out of the fresh concrete, moisten the soil before shovelling the concrete into place.

7 If you need to step the concrete slightly at any point, use loosely laid bricks to hold the wet mixture in place while it sets. Here the bench and table foundation is higher than that cast for the wall and piers. Compact and level the concrete thoroughly.

8 When building planters, it is vital to provide drainage of some sort. A simple solution is to position several bricks at the base of the structure before placing the concrete. For larger planters, simply throw strip foundations, leaving the centre open.

9 When the concrete has set, but is not yet hard, remove the bricks. If you leave them for too long, you will have to chip them out with a chisel; to prevent this happening, wiggle the bricks from time to time while the concrete is setting.

10 Remove the bricks used to step the foundation and leave the concrete to set thoroughly, at least overnight. Before you start laying the bricks, set them out on the foundations, without any mortar, to check the layout you have planned.

11 This shows the position of the central pier which will support the timber used to create seating. Because it is stepped above the first course of the wall, one extra brick will be needed alongside the wall to support it.

12 A section of the wall is included in the design at one end. If you are not building a screen wall, the back of the structure will simply be lower, in keeping with height of the planters and table, and the pier will not be included.

13　The storage box and adjacent table area are set out against an existing wall and pillar. Every site will differ and there is no reason that these features should not be free-standing. Alternatively, you could build a low wall behind the box to form a backrest.

14　Mark the position of the loose bricks with chalk or pencil, then remove them. Mix mortar in the required ratio and start laying the bricks at any one of the corners, as described in steps 9–16 on page 42. Make sure the first brick is level.

15　The first course must also be square. Use the correct tools to check the angles and to make absolutely sure that the upper surface of the first course is flat and level. To do this, set the spirit level at various angles along the tops of the bricks.

16　Do not assume that any existing walls or features are square and plumb. Rather check your own brickwork regularly. If the walls of this storage box are not laid accurately, you will have problems fitting the lid at a later stage.

17　There are various ways to build pillars and piers. This 340 mm x 340 mm pillar is constructed with four bricks, so that it can bond with the half brick wall. Lay the first course of bricks on a bed of mortar and use a spirit level to check that they are flat.

18　You can leave the central core hollow, or, if the pillar is relatively high, insert a reinforcing rod through the centre and fill the hollow with mortar or a weak concrete mix, This pillar is built with a half brick in the centre, making it reasonably solid.

19　Make sure that the brickwork is square before you go any further. Here, the wall continues from the pillar. This will ensure that the bricks bond well, but the effect of a running stretcher bond will be interrupted by a half brick at times.

20　Continue to lay the first course of all the features. The configuration of the table follows a paving stack bond at this stage; the next course will be laid so that all the bricks in this part of the structure bond properly and do not fall over.

21　Once the first course of bricks is in place, you can start laying the next course, preferably at a corner. If there is a wide expanse of wall, use a spirit level to align this first, and then use it as a datum point for the rest of brickwork at this level.

22 Then move to the next corner, align the two outside bricks, and string a builder's line at the correct height. Then lay bricks between the corners to complete the course. Be sure to bond the bricks to form a half-brick wall in stretcher bond.

23 When you lay the second course of the table adjoining the planters, you will need to cut some of the bricks to ensure the structure is properly bonded. You cannot just lay them in the opposite direction as there will be a gap through the middle.

24 The central pier which will form a support for the bench must also be built using stretcher bond, even though this little wall is only five courses high. Lay the first brick of the second course across the front of the two parallel bricks in the first course.

25 Knock the bricks into place with the handle of the trowel and then check the corners again with the builder's square. Use the spirit level to make sure the brickwork at each end is properly aligned with the central pier. It will be difficult to rectify faults later.

26 It is important to create weepholes at the base of the wall to allow water to drain from the patio. The simplest method is to leave some of the vertical joints unmortared. These holes will be just above ground level once paving is laid.

27 Use a pin and builder's line to keep the courses straight. Push the pin into the wet mortar one course below the one you are laying, and pull the line around the corner at an angle. Wind the line around a loose brick to keep it in place at the other end.

28 Even if you are buttering one end of each brick (see step 13 on page 43), you will find that you need to add mortar to some of the joints. Put a little mortar on the trowel and cut gently into the joint with the edge of the tool, tapping it slightly.

29 The stepped planters are built up three and five courses above the eventual level of the paved patio. The supporting pier for the bench is one course lower than the table surface which is incorporated alongside the two planters.

30 When creating a solid brick surface, a good tip from the professionals is to lay the outside bricks before filling in the centre. This helps to keep the vertical surfaces plumb. Take care not to shift the outer bricks when you lay those in the middle.

31 Follow the same procedure when building the larger table adjacent to the wall at the other end. Make sure that each course bonds with the one beneath it, and finish the table area one course higher than the supporting pier for the bench.

32 Continue building the screen wall to the required height. You will need to string a line along the entire length of the wall to keep the brick courses straight. It is a good idea to use a gauge rod now and then to check that all the joints are even.

33 If any portion of the brickwork is to be rendered, this can be done once the mortar used to lay the bricks has set. Mix a new batch of mortar and lay it onto your surface with a plasterer's trowel, applying enough pressure to make it stick to the bricks.

34 The render should be between 10 mm and 15 mm thick. Leave it while it begins to set, then, after about an hour, use a straight-edged length of wood or a spirit level to scrape and smooth the surface. Accuracy is not important.

35 Once the surface is reasonably smooth, use a wooden float to create a more even finish. Use an even pressure and a regular wrist movement, but do not over-trowel or the finer material will come to the surface and may cause cracking.

36 The next step is to finish table tops and all other exposed horizontal brick surfaces with pavers. Where the rendered surface meets a facebrick wall, you should use the spirit level to ensure that the pavers are level on the vertical plane.

37 Once the first paver is in position, you can lay the rest of the bricks around the lip of the higher planter and on the surface of the smaller table top. Bed the pavers in mortar and butter one side and one end before pushing into place.

38 Then lay paving bricks around the top of the lower planter, first filling in any holes with mortar. Place a sausage of mortar on the upper surface and create a slight furrow with the trowel in exactly the same way as you would to lay ordinary bricks.

39 Place the first paving brick in position and check that it is level. Butter the end of the second paver and push it into place. Then use your spirit level again, and tap any uneven bricks with a rubber mallet until they are absolutely flat and level.

40 When you have completed the planters and the mortar is well set, paint a bitumen-based sealant on the inside surface. This will prevent moisture from affecting the outer skin of the brickwork. When the bitumen is dry, fill the box with soil and plant.

41 When finishing off the table top positioned in the corner between old and new walls, lay the first brick at the outer corner and ensure that both the horizontal and the vertical surfaces are plumb. Make sure that the joints are neat and tidy.

42 Place an even bed of mortar on the upper surface of the brickwork. Then butter the sides of the bricks as you lay the outer row. Knock each one gently into place with a mallet and check that they are all level with one another.

43 Butter both the length and the top of each of the bricks laid on the inner row of the table top. There will be a slight gap between the edge of the pavers and the wall. This can be filled with mortar, using a trowel to make sure that it is level with the pavers.

44 Once the table top is complete, you may find that some of the joints need to be filled (or pointed). It will also be necessary to neaten the joints with a special trowel or jointer. Those without specialist tools could use a piece of metal instead.

45 Make the seat for the bench by screwing four 450 mm x 70 mm x 45 mm wide slats across six 2.5 m lengths. Position them so that there is one short piece on either side of the central brick pier, and one on the inside of each of the end piers.

46 The back rest is made with four 70 mm wide lengths of timber which are screwed to the wall. This will prevent a textured facebrick finish from scraping against you or damaging clothing. It also creates the impression of more substantial built-in furniture.

47 Make the storage box lid from a 1.5 m x 710 mm sheet of exterior plywood and nine 1.5 m x 70 mm wide slats. Cut five shallow channels across the width of the slats. Glue them to one side of the plywood then, working from the other side, tack the slats down.

48 Glue and screw four slats, 700 mm long and 20 mm thick, across the board, using 50 mm long screws to secure each of the nine seating slats. Screw brass hinges to the lid, then attach it to the wall with appropriate screws and Rawl plugs.

DESIGNS AND PLANS

An attractive and useful storage box with a hinged lid doubles as a bench on a compact but much used patio. Large enough to house cushions and other bulky items which might be damaged by rain, it is built on a solid concrete slab, and against an existing wall, which is not shown on the illustration. You will require an additional 39 bricks as well as an extra 10 kg of cement and sand for mortar if you need to construct the back wall of a freestanding storage box. Facebricks should be used to build the basic structure, while any good quality timber recommended for exterior use may be used for the lid. If a soft wood (like pine) is chosen, it may be necessary to use thicker slats to prevent any possible buckling.

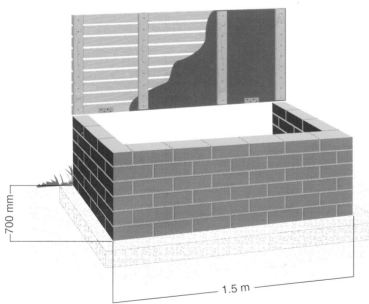

MATERIALS

Foundation
30 kg cement
122 kg sand
122 kg stone

Brickwork
72 facebricks
 (+ 39 if required)
25 kg cement
 (+ 10 kg if required)
12.5 kg lime
 (optional)
100 kg sand
 (+ 10 kg if required)

Lid
1.5 m x 710 mm x 6 mm
 sheet exterior-grade
 plywood
9 x 1.5 m x 70 mm x 40 mm
 slats
4 x 700 mm x 70 mm
 x 20 mm crosspieces
15 mm panel pins
36 x 50 mm brass screws
2 brass butt hinges with
 brass screws and Rawl
 plugs
waterproof wood glue

1 Measure and mark a 1.6 m x 800 mm area for the foundation. Dig to a depth of 100 mm; then compact and level the ground.
2 Mix the concrete and place over the foundation area. Allow to set overnight.
3 Lay the brick walls of the box using stretcher bond. Allow the mortar to set thoroughly.
4 Meanwhile, assemble the lid. First cut five shallow channels across the width of each of the 1.5 m slats to aid drainage. Then position these lengths, with the grooves

facing upward, on a solid surface so that you have 10 mm gaps between each. Glue and tack the plywood on top using a good quality waterproof wood glue and panel pins. When the glue is dry, position the four 700 mm crosspieces evenly across the ply, so that those at each end are flush with the edges. Glue and then screw through the timber to secure the slats.
5 When the glue is completely dry and the mortar thoroughly set, screw the hinges to the lid and then affix to the wall using screws and Rawl plugs.

Plain, goodlooking and easy to build, this raised and freestanding planter will add visual interest to any patio. Furthermore, its dimensions are easily altered and it could be increased in size to suit the style and shape of your paved outdoor area. Although this planter can be built on a strip foundation, it is simpler to throw a slab, placing bricks on the ground and then removing them to create instant drainage holes once the concrete has almost set. With a structure this size, wastage of concrete is minimal. If you are building on an existing patio, you will need to chop out some of the bricks to enable water to drain away.

MATERIALS

Foundation
20 kg cement
80 kg sand
80 kg stone

Brickwork
66 facebricks
11 paving bricks
20 kg cement
10 kg lime (optional)
80 kg sand

1 Measure out an area 800 mm x 1 m and peg out. Dig a 100 mm deep foundation.
2 Mix the concrete and, before laying, set two or three bricks in the centre of the proposed structure. Lay the slab and allow the concrete to set. Before it becomes totally hard, remove the bricks.
3 Start laying the bricks using stretcher bond. Create weepholes in the second course by excluding every second vertical joint. Piping can be inserted if more substantial drainage is required.
4 Lay as many courses as required and top with a final course of pavers.
5 If you wish, seal the interior walls of the planter with a bitumen-based product to prevent future discolouration of the bricks by constant moisture.

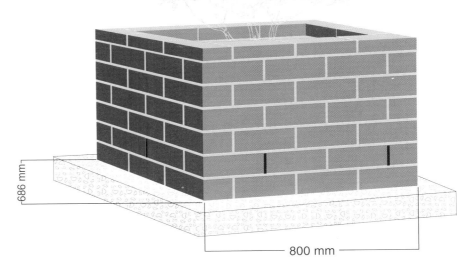

686 mm

800 mm

Delightfully rustic seating alongside the house not only provides a resting place, but also adds character to the plain wall. Simple to build, this is a perfect weekend project for the DIYer. These two seats are built from facebrick, but the same design could be rendered and painted. Although quantities specified call for a solid concrete core in each seat, you can save on materials by filling the central gap with sand to about the height of the fourth brick course, compacting well and then topping with concrete.

MATERIALS

Foundations
20 kg cement
80 kg sand
80 kg stone

Brickwork
60 bricks
15 kg cement
7.5 kg lime (optional)
60 kg sand

Woodwork
6 x 125 mm x 22 mm
  x 500 mm for seats
6 x 70 mm x 22 mm
  x 500 mm for back rests
36 x 40 mm brass screws
  with Rawl plugs

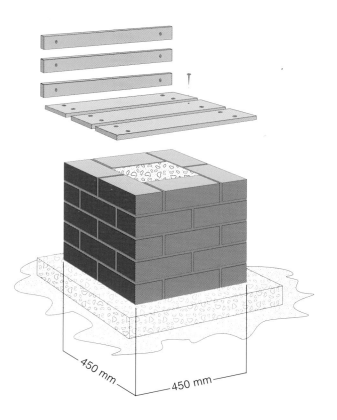

1 Measure out the two seats and peg the area required for foundations. Dig to a depth of 100 mm.
2 Mix half the concrete and lay the slab. Allow to set thoroughly overnight.
3 Build the base plinth using stretcher bond. Leave until the mortar has set.
4 Mix a new batch of concrete and place in the centre of the brickwork. Compact well and level the upper surface.
5 When the concrete is well set, screw the seat timbers to the side walls, using two screws at the ends of each board.
6 Screw the narrow back rest timbers to the adjacent wall, ensuring they are evenly spaced.

An attractive corner planter not only adds interest to the wall, giving it a more professional finish, but it also allows for visual access, which is particularly important at busy street corners. Built with precast concrete blocks, this design is part of a rendered wall and most appropriate if used around the boundary of a property. As the structure is outside the garden itself, it is advisable to choose shrubs and plants which will not demand much maintenance. Materials specified will allow you to build the wall and planter plus about 3.5 m of wall on either side.

MATERIALS

Foundations
320 kg cement
1 m³ sand
1 m³ stone

Blockwork
408 x 390 mm x 190 mm x 190 mm concrete
   blocks, about 40 halved and broken
135 kg cement
68 kg lime (optional)
0.65 m³ sand

Mortar for rendering
320 kg cement
160 kg lime (optional)
1.6 m³ sand

1 Mark out the position of the wall and planter as illustrated, leaving the base of the planter untouched.
2 Dig the foundation trenches to a depth of at least 250 mm.
3 Mix the concrete in a cement:sand:stone ratio of 1:4:4 with water and place in the trenches. Compact, level and leave to set overnight.
4 Build the wall and planter using stretcher bond. The planter should be four courses high and the wall itself 12 courses.

5 Use half blocks and broken pieces to build the capping along the top.
6 Once the mortar has set, render the wall and finish off the capping to create a neat, sloping finish as illustrated.
7 When the mortar has set and is completely dry, paint the wall.

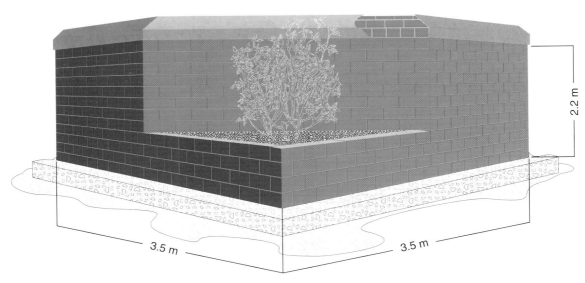

2.2 m

3.5 m   3.5 m

This practical screen wall is built on a curve to add character to a patio or utility area. The adjacent seat, which curves alongside the wall, may be used as a resting spot or to display pot plants. Although this design has been roughly bagged with cement to give it a rustic feel, it could also be rendered for a more formal effect, or built with facebricks to match the walls of the house. The seat has been topped with tiles to finish it off; if facebricks are used for construction, paving bricks may be a better option. The materials listed will allow you to build the seat and a 1.2 m high wall which is about 3.2 m long.

MATERIALS

Foundations
70 kg cement
280 kg sand
280 kg stone

Brickwork
437 bricks
24 brick-sized tiles
   (or paving bricks)
150 kg cement
75 kg lime (optional)
600 kg sand

1 Measure the line the wall will follow and peg out the foundations as shown on the illustration. Measure and peg out the area required for the adjacent seat. Dig to a depth of 250 mm. Compact and level the earth.
2 Mix the concrete and lay the foundation for both wall and seat. Allow the concrete to set before continuing with the brickwork.
3 Lay the bricks for the one-brick wall first, using an English bond with alternate courses of headers and stretchers. Then lay the bricks for the seat. Allow the mortar to set.
4 If desired, mix a small amount of mortar, adding more water than usual, and smear the mixture onto the wall with sacking to achieve a thin, 'bagged' finish.
5 Once all the mortar has set thoroughly, top the seat with tiles as illustrated, cutting those at the back to fit. Paint the structure.

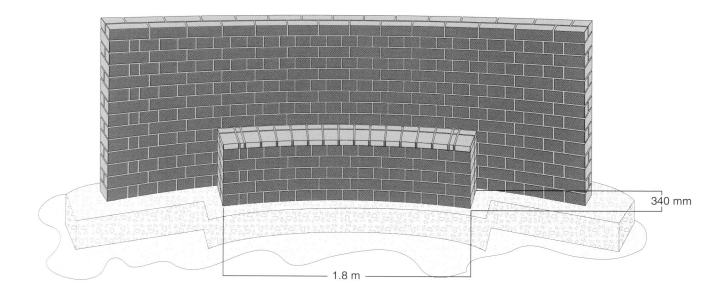

340 mm

1.8 m

An elegant, period-style bench can be constructed in the garden by anyone with basic bricklaying skills. Smoothly rendered with a mortar mix and then painted, it will soon look like a beautifully sculpted piece of garden furniture. This design is built with ordinary bricks, using the simple stretcher bond. The central cavity, which forms the seat of the structure, may be filled with rubble, even though materials here call for sand. Whatever material is used must be well compacted before being topped with a layer of concrete, which is skimmed with mortar to create a smooth finish.

MATERIALS

Foundations
100 kg cement
405 kg sand
405 kg stone

Brickwork
207 bricks
50 kg cement
25 kg lime (optional)
200 kg sand

Mortar for rendering
20 kg cement
10 kg lime (optional)
80 kg sand

Seating slab
0.6 m³ sand or fill
15 kg cement
60 kg sand
60 kg stone

1 Choose the position of the seat and peg out a rectangle 2.2 m x 1.2 m. Excavate to a depth of about 150 mm.
2 Mix the concrete in the ratio 1:4:4 and then lay to create a slab foundation. Allow to set thoroughly – at least overnight.
3 Build the walls to form the basic structure of the seat, as illustrated.
4 When the mortar has set, fill the central cavity with sand or fill. Compact well.
5 Mix the concrete for the seating slab and lay over the compacted sand. Leave to set thoroughly.
6 Finally, render the outside walls of the structure with a 1:4 mortar mix, filling in all gaps between the bricks.

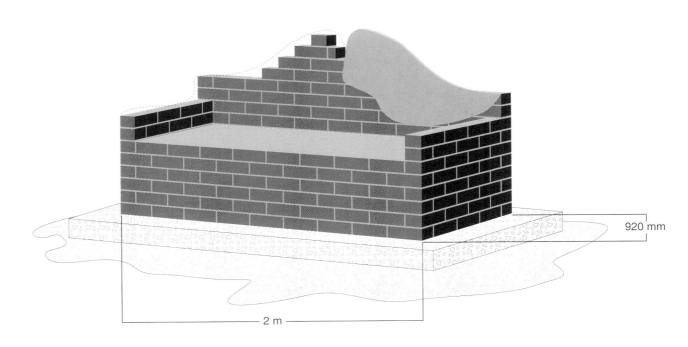

920 mm

2 m

This unusual arched planter has been built as a feature in a 2.65 m high garden boundary wall. While the central panel has simply been lightly bagged with a cement/sand slush, the curved wall and surrounding trim have been neatly rendered for effect. Decorated with a precast gargoyle and bowl, and planted with colourful annuals, this design will brighten a dull spot in any garden, big or small. If built on a solid concrete slab and properly waterproofed, it could even be adapted as a pond. Quantities specified do not include brickwork for the adjacent wall or its foundations.

MATERIALS

Foundation
50 kg cement
200 kg sand
200 kg stone

Brickwork
345 bricks
90 kg cement
45 kg lime (optional)
360 kg sand

Render
20 kg cement
10 kg lime (optional)
80 kg sand

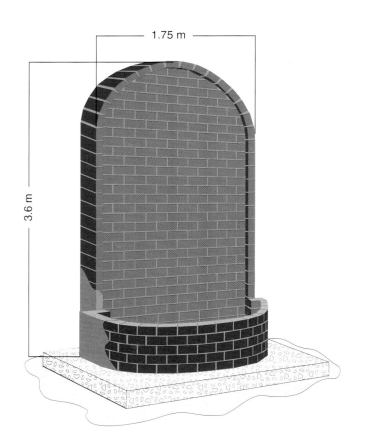

1.75 m

3.6 m

1 Measure and peg out the area required for the planter. Dig trenches for strip foundations to a depth of 250 mm; compact and level the earth.
2 Mix the concrete in a 1:4:4 cement:sand:stone ratio and place in the trenches. Allow to set thoroughly, at least overnight.
3 Unless the structure is to be freestanding, lay the back wall as illustrated, tying in to the garden wall. The first 26 courses require seven bricks in each course; thereafter, use a half brick less in each of the next four courses, and reduce by a full brick in the two top courses. Cut the bricks where necessary to achieve the arched effect.
4 Allow the mortar to set thoroughly. The surrounding trim may then be laid, using bricks on edge. These will protrude at the back and front of the wall.
5 Mix mortar in a 1:4 ratio for the render and finish off the trim and front wall. Add water to what is left of the mix and smear over the back wall with sacking.
6 When all the render has set, paint the structure, then attach a gargoyle and decorative planter bowl, if desired.
7 Fill the planter with soil, and plant.

This sleek but simple barbecue design incorporates seating on the perimeter of a brick paved patio. Built from face-bricks, it has a sophisticated appeal which will suit the more formal garden plan. The pillar on one side may be used as a table, and there is room for storage of wood under the cooking surface. Although the materials specified call for a fibrecement pipe to help remove smoke from the chimney, a metal pipe may be used instead.

MATERIALS

Foundation
130 kg cement
520 kg sand
520 kg stone

Brickwork
514 bricks
50 paving bricks
175 kg cement

85 kg lime (optional)
0.85 m³ sand (including
  0.35 m³ for fill)
650 mm x 114 mm x 75 mm
  concrete lintel
600 mm x 600 mm x 50 mm
  concrete slab
1.8 m x 150 mm fibrecement
  pipe

1 Measure and peg out the area where the barbecue and seating are to be located. Excavate for a 250 mm slab foundation.
2 Mix and place the concrete. Leave to set.
3 Build up the walls as illustrated, using the slab to span the lower section of the barbecue structure. Leave the core of the left-hand pillar and the area below the seating hollow, and use paving bricks for the top course of the pillar.
4 Build the lintel across the front of the base of the chimney. Set the pipe behind the front chimney wall and build into the brickwork. Allow the mortar to set.
5 Fill the hollow areas with sand and compact. Top with paving bricks.

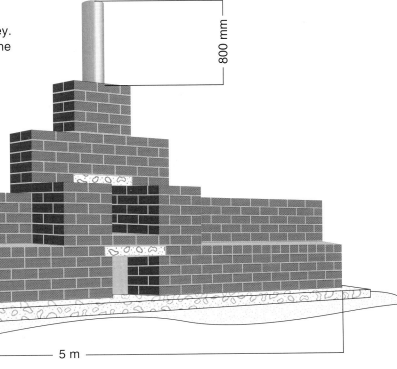

This lovely traditional water feature may be constructed as a freestanding structure or built into a wall. Although this one was built using precast concrete materials, the illustration will enable you to build it with bricks. As the pool must be waterproof, you should use stronger concrete and mortar mixes than those specified for ordinary garden structures. Avoid using toxic lime, especially if you plan to stock the pond with fish. You may, if you wish, incorporate corbels at the sides instead of the low side walls, and top the three-brick-high front wall with swimming pool coping instead of a rendered lip. The wall-mounted fountain is an attractive optional feature which will add an element of movement to the pond. Any fountain-head or gargoyle may be used and this can spurt directly into the pool or into a bowl set on the lip.

MATERIALS

Foundation
375 kg cement
0.55 m³ (750 kg) sand
0.55 m³ (750 kg) stone

Brickwork
570 bricks
160 kg cement
480 kg sand

Render
175 kg cement
waterproofing additive (optional)
525 kg sand

Fountain and accessories (optional)
Precast fountain-head or gargoyle
2.2 m tubing, 12 mm in diameter
2 elbow connectors, internal
  diameter 12 mm
Submersible pump with
  1.8 m water head
Outdoor cable
  and conduit

1 Measure out the area required for the structure. Peg and excavate a 475 mm deep trench to accommodate a 250 mm deep foundation and two brick courses. Compact the base.
2 Mix concrete in a cement:sand:stone ratio of 1:2:2 and place in the trench. Level and compact it; allow to set well.
3 Build up the brick walls and side pillars according to the illustrations, using a 1:3 cement:sand mix. The first nine courses of the back wall are double courses; from the shelf upwards, build a half-brick wall. If precast materials are to be used, secure them with mortar.
4 When the mortar has set, fill in the upper section of the trench with soil.
5 Chase a channel in the wall for pipework. Chip out with a cold chisel to a depth of about 20 mm.

6 Route the cabling to the pond, either through the pond wall or over the edge. Seal with silicone if necessary. Run the cable to an outside weatherproof box and connect to the electricity supply.
7 Cut off two 100 mm lengths of tubing and join them to the longer length with elbow connectors. Push into the channel and allow to extend at either end.
8 Render the entire structure, creating lips and indentations as required.
9 Once the rendered surface has set thoroughly, attach one end of the pipe to the pump and push the other end through the hole in the fountain-head.
10 Paint several coats of rubberised bitumen or any other sealant onto the inside of the pond, following the manufacturer's instructions.
11 Paint the rest of the structure.

2 m

2.5 m

1.4 m

2.35 m

A charming, arched brick entrance, well within the
capabilities of any competent DIY bricklayer, ties in to the
boundary wall and incorporates two attractive planters. The
generous proportions of the arch itself give the entrance an
air of stature, suitable for both small and larger properties.
Materials specified for this structure – which could also be
rendered and painted rather than built in facebrick – do not
include adjacent walls. Any additional brickwork you may
wish to construct can be quickly quantified from the
instructions provided on pages 35–36.

MATERIALS

Foundation
70 kg cement
280 kg sand
280 kg stone

Brickwork
670 bricks
225 kg cement
112 kg lime (optional)
0.67 m³ (900 kg) sand

1 Peg out the foundations and dig to a
depth of 250 mm. Compact and level
the soil.
2 Place a few bricks at the base of the
planters (see page 47). Mix concrete in
a cement:sand:stone ratio of 1:4:4 and
place in the excavated trench. Allow to
set partially, then remove the bricks
and leave overnight.
3 Build up the walls, leaving a gap as

wide as the length of a brick between
the single-brick, 24-course-high back
wall and the half-brick, eight-course-
high front wall of the planter.
4 Build up the arch, using formwork
made from chipboard and hardboard
to support the brickwork.
5 Top the front of the planters with a
soldier course of bricks and the back
wall with a header course.

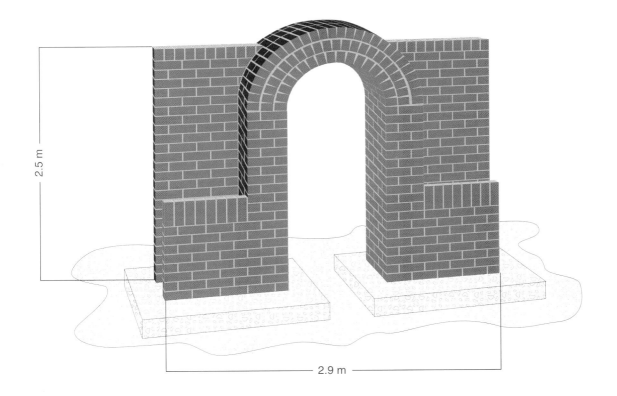

2.5 m

2.9 m

METRIC/IMPERIAL CONVERSION TABLE

To convert the measurements given in this book to imperial measurements, simply multiply the figure given in the text by the relevant number shown in the table alongside. Bear in mind that conversions will not necessarily work out exactly, and you will need to round the figure up or down slightly. (Do not use a combination of metric and imperial measurements – for accuracy, rather stick to one or the other system.)

TO CONVERT	MULTIPLY BY
millimetres to inches	0.0394
metres to feet	3.28
metres to yards	1.093
sq millimetres to sq inches	0.00155
sq metres to sq feet	10.76
sq metres to sq yards	1.195
cu metres to cu feet	35.31
cu metres to cu yards	1.308
grams to pounds	0.0022
kilograms to pounds	2.2046
litres to gallons	0.22

UNITED KINGDOM

B&Q plc
Portswood House
Hampshire Corporate Park
Chandlers Ford
Eastleigh
Hants S03 3YX
Tel: (01703) 256256
(Branches throughout the UK)

Brick Development Association
Woodside House
Winkfield, Windsor, Berks SL4 2DX
Tel: (01344) 885651

Building Centre Group
26 Store Street, London WC1E 7BT
Tel: (0171) 637 1022 (Technical advice)
Tel: (01344) 884999 (Useful literature)
(Also in Bristol, Glasgow and
Manchester)

Do-It-All
Falcon House
The Minories
Dudley, West Midlands DY2 8PG
Tel: (01384) 456456
(Branches throughout the UK)

Homebase Ltd
Beddington House
Wallington, Surrey SM6 0HB
Tel: (0181) 784 7200
(Branches throughout the UK)

Jewson Ltd
Intwood Road
Cringleford, Norwich NR4 UXB
Tel: (01603) 456133
(Branches throughout the UK)

Onduline Building Products
(organic-fibre roof sheeting)
Eadley Place, 182–184 Campden Hill Road
Kensington, London W8 7AS
Tel: (0171) 7277 0533

Texas Homecare
Homecharm House
Parkfarm, Wellingborough
Northampton NN5 7UG
Tel: (01933) 679679
(Branches throughout the UK)

Travis Perkins
Lodge Way House
Lodge Way
Harlestone Road
Northampton NN5 7UG
Tel: (01604) 752424
(Branches throughout the UK)

Wickes
120–138 Station Road
Harrow
Middlesex HA1 2QB
Tel: (0181) 863 5696
(Branches throughout the UK)

SOUTH AFRICA

Buildex
433 Commissioner Street
Johannesburg
Tel: (011) 614 3786/3545

The Building Centre
209 Cartwrights Corner
Adderley Street 8001
Cape Town
Tel: (021) 461 6095/1121

**Building Industries' Federation
of South Africa (Bifsa)**
234 Alexandra Avenue
Halfway House 1685
Tel: (011) 315 1010

Clay Brick Association
Old Pretoria Road
Halfway House 1685
Tel: (011) 805 4206

**Concrete Society of Southern
Africa/Portland Cement Institute (PCI)**
Head office: Portland Park
Halfway House
P O Box 168, Halfway House 1685
Tel: (011) 315 0300; fax: (011) 315 0584
Regional offices:
P O Box 13019, Humewood 6013
Tel: (041) 53 2141; fax: (041) 53 3496
P O Box 12, Vrijzee 7495
Tel: (021) 591 5234; fax: (021) 591 3502
P O Box 1393, Wandsbeck 3631
Tel: (031) 86 1306/7; fax: (031) 86 7241

Corobrik
P O Box 1517, Durban 4000
Tel: (031) 560 3111; fax: (031) 84 6752
P O Box 49, Germiston 1400
Tel: (011) 871 8600; fax: (011) 45 3221
P O Box 38, Stellenbosch 7599
Tel: (021) 887 3311; fax: (021) 887 2766
P O Box 20, Swartkops 6210
Tel: (041) 66 2701; fax: (041) 66 2704

**Natal Master Builders' and Allied Industries'
Association Exhibition Centre**
40 Essex Terrace
Westville, KwaZulu-Natal
Tel: (031) 86 7070

AUSTRALIA

Adelaide Paving Centre
Alexandrina Road
Mount Barker, South Australia 5251
Tel: 1800 625 500

Atlas Brick and Paving Centre
Alexandra Drive
Noranda, Western Australia 6062
Tel: (08) 9249 1422
(5 branches in Western Australia)

BBC Hardware
Head Office: Building A
Cnr Cambridge & Chester Streets
Epping, NSW 2121
Tel: (02) 9876 0888
(Branches throughout Australia)

Bunnings Building Supplies
Head Office:
152 Pilbara Street
Welshpool, Western Australia 6106
Tel: (08) 9365 1555
(24 branches in Western Australia)

Harcros Timber & Building Supplies
Head Office:
586 Doncaster Road
Doncaster, Victoria 3108
Tel: (03) 9848 7577
(5 branches in Victoria)

Hudson Timber and Hardware
Head Office:
Cnr Showground Road & Victoria Avenue
Castle Hill, NSW 2154
Tel: (02) 9534 5344
(10 branches in NSW)

Marion Sand & Metal Paving Centre
917 Marion Road
Mitchell Park, South Australia 5043
Tel: (08) 8296 5122

Mitre 10
Head Office:
1367 Main North Road
Para Hills West, South Australia 5096
Tel: (08) 8281 2244

Terraforce
Head Office: Boral Besser
P O Box 6, Seven Hills, NSW 2147
Tel: (02) 9896 4222
(Branches throughout Australia)

NEW ZEALAND

Terraforce
P O Box 3910, Auckland